AMERICAN
SOCIAL
MOVEMENTS

THE FREE
SPEECH
MOVEMENT

Bradley Steffens, *Book Editor*

Bruce Glassman, *Vice President*
Bonnie Szumski, *Publisher*
Helen Cothran, *Managing Editor*

GREENHAVEN
PRESS®

THOMSON
GALE

San Diego • Detroit • New York • San Francisco • Cleveland
New Haven, Conn. • Waterville, Maine • London • Munich

LIBRARY OF CONGRESS CATALOGING-IN-PUBLICATION DATA

The free speech movement / Bradley Steffens, book editor.
   p. cm. — (American social movements)
Includes bibliographical references and index.
ISBN 0-7377-1156-6 (lib. : alk. paper)
   1. Freedom of speech—United States—History. I. Steffens, Bradley, 1955– .
II. Series.
KF4772.F738 2004
342.7308'53—dc22
                                     2003064686

Printed in the United States of America

CONTENTS

Foreword   7

Introduction: Fighting for Free Speech   9

Chapter 1 • PHILOSOPHICAL ORIGINS

Speech Is Self-Regulating   23
by John Milton
> The author of *Paradise Lost* argues that the role of government is not to suppress speech it deems undesirable, but to create an environment in which ideas—good and bad alike—can compete freely.

The Rights of Individuals   29
by William Blackstone
> The author of a renowned commentary on English law argues against prior restraints on speech but allows for the punishment of those who use expression to violate the rights of others.

Social Liberty   35
by John Stuart Mill
> The British philosopher argues that the liberties of thought and expression are absolute rights that must be protected not only from interference by the government but also from coercion by public opinion.

Chapter 2 • THE FIRST AMENDMENT AND CONSTITUTIONAL FREE SPEECH

The Limits of Free Speech   44
by Joseph Story
> A U.S. Supreme Court justice examines the origins of the First Amendment and argues that the guarantees of free speech and a free press are not absolute.

The Original Intent of the First Amendment   53
by Stanley C. Brubaker
> A noted First Amendment scholar suggests that the

framers did not intend for the First Amendment to be a guiding principle for democracy.

The Supreme Court and the States Apply the First Amendment 69
by Frede Castberg
A professor and rector at the University of Oslo examines several high court decisions that effectively erased restrictions on speech and the press.

Chapter 3 • LANDMARK SUPREME COURT DECISIONS

The Doctrine of Incitement 77
by Oliver Wendell Holmes Jr.
A Supreme Court justice declares that a speaker who incites lawless action is not protected by the First Amendment.

The Right of the State to Protect Itself 82
by Felix Frankfurter
A Supreme Court justice cautions against taking the language of the First Amendment literally. Instead, he calls for an interpretation of the Constitution as a living document that derives its meaning from historical circumstances.

Restricting Pornography Violates the First Amendment 95
by William O. Douglas
An associate justice of the Supreme Court challenges the validity of the Court's finding that obscene expression is not protected by the First Amendment.

Offensive Speech Is Protected by the First Amendment 102
by William Brennan Jr.
Writing for the majority of the Court, Justice Brennan explains why burning an American flag is protected expression under the First Amendment.

Chapter 4 • FREE SPEECH AS A SOCIAL MOVEMENT

The Alien and Sedition Acts of 1798　　　115
by Nat Hentoff
> A noted columnist and author recounts how the
> passage of the Alien and Sedition Acts of 1798
> criminalized some speech, creating a constitutional
> crisis.

The Struggle for Free Speech in the Civil War　122
by Michael Kent Curtis
> A professor of constitutional law describes how
> President Abraham Lincoln's wartime proclamation
> establishing martial law and outlawing "any disloyal
> practice, affording aid and comfort to Rebels" re-
> sulted in the arrest, conviction, and banishment of
> an outspoken critic of the Civil War.

**The American Civil Liberties Union Fights
for Free Speech**　　　140
by Samuel Walker
> A longtime member of the American Civil Liber-
> ties Union (ACLU) explains how Roger Baldwin
> was moved by government crackdowns on World
> War I protesters and other dissidents to abandon his
> career in social work and found an organization de-
> voted to defending civil liberties.

The Berkeley Free Speech Movement　　　156
by David Burner
> A political historian recounts how the weeks of pro-
> test at the University of California, Berkeley, led to a
> relaxation of regulations on speech, changing cam-
> pus life not only at Berkeley but across the nation.

Chapter 5 • CONTEMPORARY FREE SPEECH CONTROVERSIES

Free Speech and Sexual Harassment　　　172
by Deborah Ellis
> The legal director for the National Organization for

Women Legal Defense and Education Fund examines the problem of sexually harassing speech in the workplace.

The Problem of Limiting Pornography and Hate Speech   179
by Nicholas Wolfson
A professor of law describes how the right to free speech is being challenged by individuals who traditionally have supported it: feminists and members of minority groups.

Regulating Speech on College Campuses   185
by Timothy C. Shiell
A professor of philosophy proposes essential criteria for developing narrowly drawn speech codes that can regulate hate speech without infringing on free speech as a whole.

Free Speech and the Internet   197
by Joshua Micah Marshall
A noted journalist describes how software filters, which allow Internet users to limit their exposure to offensive materials, present hidden dangers to free speech.

Chronology   **208**
For Further Research   **213**
Index   **217**

FOREWORD

Historians Gary T. Marx and Douglas McAdam define a social movement as "organized efforts to promote or resist change in society that rely, at least in part, on noninstitutionalized forms of political action." Examining American social movements broadens and vitalizes the study of history by allowing students to observe the efforts of ordinary individuals and groups to oppose the established values of their era, often in unconventional ways. The civil rights movement of the twentieth century, for example, began as an effort to challenge legalized racial segregation and garner social and political rights for African Americans. Several grassroots organizations—groups of ordinary citizens committed to social activism—came together to organize boycotts, sit-ins, voter registration drives, and demonstrations to counteract racial discrimination. Initially, the movement faced massive opposition from white citizens, who had long been accustomed to the social standards that required the separation of the races in almost all areas of life. But the movement's consistent use of an innovative form of protest—nonviolent direct action—eventually aroused the public conscience, which in turn paved the way for major legislative victories such as the Civil Rights Act of 1964 and the Voting Rights Act of 1965. Examining the civil rights movement reveals how ordinary people can use nonstandard political strategies to change society.

Investigating the style, tactics, personalities, and ideologies of American social movements also encourages students to learn about aspects of history and culture that may receive scant attention in textbooks. As scholar Eric Foner notes, American history "has been constructed not only in congressional debates and political treatises, but also on plantations and picket lines, in parlors and bedrooms. Frederick Douglass, Eugene V. Debs, and Margaret Sanger . . . are its architects as well as Thomas Jefferson and Abraham Lincoln." While not all

American social movements garner popular support or lead to epoch-changing legislation, they each offer their own unique insight into a young democracy's political dialogue.

Each book in Greenhaven's American Social Movements series allows readers to follow the general progression of a particular social movement—examining its historical roots and beginnings in earlier chapters and relatively recent and contemporary information (or even the movement's demise) in later chapters. With the incorporation of both primary and secondary sources, as well as writings by both supporters and critics of the movement, each anthology provides an engaging panoramic view of its subject. Selections include a variety of readings, such as book excerpts, newspaper articles, speeches, manifestos, literary essays, interviews, and personal narratives. The editors of each volume aim to include the voices of movement leaders and participants as well as the opinions of historians, social analysts, and individuals who have been affected by the movement. This comprehensive approach gives students the opportunity to view these movements both as participants have experienced them and as historians and critics have interpreted them.

Every volume in the American Social Movements series includes an introductory essay that presents a broad historical overview of the movement in question. The annotated table of contents and comprehensive index help readers quickly locate material of interest. Each selection is preceded by an introductory paragraph that summarizes the article's content and provides historical context when necessary. Several other research aids are also present, including brief excerpts of supplementary material, a chronology of major events pertaining to the movement, and an accessible bibliography.

The Greenhaven Press American Social Movements series offers readers an informative introduction to some of the most fascinating groups and ideas in American history. The contents of each anthology provide a valuable resource for general readers as well as for enthusiasts of American political science, history, and culture.

Fighting for Free Speech

The struggle for free speech typically pits the right of the individual to express himself or herself against the right of society to maintain order. Such conflicts, however, are rare. Most communication serves both the individual and society, helping to facilitate the distribution of goods, to improve security, to promote cultural advancement, and achieve other group goals. As a result, many societies worldwide encourage open discussion through commerce, education, entertainment, and political debate. Based on the universality of such practices, anthropologists theorize that even prehistoric societies created settings in which their members could exchange information.

Not all speech benefits society, however. A speaker can disrupt the social order by threatening other people, making false accusations, obtaining property under false pretenses, giving away vital security information, or committing other speech-related misdeeds. As a result, every culture in every age has punished speech that infringes on individual rights, creates social turmoil, or threatens the very existence of a society.

Restraints on speech often extend beyond simple criminal conduct, however. In many religious societies, speakers who did not show proper respect for deities were punished for fear that their blasphemies might anger the gods. The leaders of many societies have prohibited speech that criticized them or their policies. Since social norms and taboos are designed to maintain the status quo, many individuals have been penalized simply for challenging prevailing beliefs or pressing for social change.

Early written laws placed limits on speech, leading scholars to conclude that speech restraints most likely predate recorded history. The author of the earliest known written code of laws, Hammurabi, the king of Babylonia from 1792 B.C. to 1750 B.C., forbade false accusations and other forms of malicious speech. "If any one bring an accusation of any crime before the elders, and does not prove what he has charged, he shall, if it be a capital offense charged, be put to death,"[1] reads Hammurabi's third law. The laws that the Jewish leader Moses gave his people around 1250 B.C. also included limits on speech. "Do not spread false reports," reads one of the laws of Moses. "Do not help a wicked man by being a malicious witness."[2]

Ancient societies also formalized ways to promote free speech. In the fifth century B.C. the Greek city-state of Athens, which practiced a form of democracy, encouraged citizens to speak out on public issues. In his play *The Suppliants*, Euripides praises the tradition of encouraging public debate: "Freedom's mark is also seen in this: 'Who has wholesome counsel to declare unto the state?' And he who chooses to do so gains renown, while he, who has no wish, remains silent. What greater equality can there be in a city?"[3]

As Euripides suggests, the public forum was reserved for constructive discourse. Harmful and offensive speech was not welcome. People who incited violence, defamed other people, or mocked the gods risked punishment, even death. The philosopher Socrates, for example, ran afoul of the government for speaking out against the Athenian constitution and promoting antidemocratic ideas. After his former students twice led successful antidemocratic revolts, Socrates was viewed with suspicion by many of his fellow citizens. After a third but unsuccessful antidemocratic uprising, the poet Meletus accused Socrates of corrupting the youth of Athens and refusing to acknowledge the gods. According to the philosopher Plato, who attended the trial of Socrates in 399 B.C., the seventy-year-old philosopher did not dispute the charges. Instead he defended himself by focusing on the positive contributions he made to society. "I do nothing but go about persuading you all, old and young alike, not to take thought for your person or your property, but first and foremost to take care of your soul, that it be as good as possible," Socrates told the jury of five hundred citizens. "This is my teaching, and if it corrupts the young, it is pernicious."[4] Rather than apologize for his beliefs, Socrates remained defiant. "While I have life and strength I shall *never* cease from the practice and teaching of philosophy,"[5] he declared. By a vote of 280 to 220 the jury found Socrates guilty, and by a vote of 360 to 140 the jurors sentenced him to death. Immortalized in painting and literature, the death of Socrates has become an icon for free speech advocates.

Protecting Church and State

The Romans, who ruled parts of Europe, Asia, and Africa from the second century B.C. to the fifth century A.D., also practiced a form of democracy and encouraged discussion among their citizens. At the same time, the Romans closely monitored what was said in public. A government official known as the *censor* enforced standards of behavior and speech within the empire—the basis for the English words "censor" and "censorship." Many Roman leaders did not tolerate criticism or dissent. When the Roman general Mark Antony became part of the ruling triumvirate in 43 B.C., he ordered his followers to hunt down and execute the orator and philosopher Cicero, who had spoken out against him before he took power. In A.D. 8 the emperor Augustus banished the poet Ovid to the far-flung outpost of Tomi for publishing works he considered immoral and licentious. And in the province of Judea, the Roman governor Pontius Pilate ordered the crucifixion of the religious leader Jesus of Nazareth for preaching doctrines that challenged the authority of Rome.

Over the next three centuries, the followers of Jesus, known as Christians, were routinely executed by Roman authorities who considered them enemies of the state. Not long after the Roman emperor Constantine became a Christian in A.D. 312, Christianity became the official religion of the Roman Empire. After the Christians came to power, they, too, tried to silence those who championed contrary beliefs. Around 496, Pope Gelasius, the leader of the church, published a decree that banned books considered theologically unsound or immoral.

Faced with an outbreak of unorthodox teachings, Pope Gregory IX created the papal Inquisition in 1231 to root out heretics. Thousands of men and women were arrested, tortured, and killed during this period of persecution. In 1633 leaders of the Roman Catholic Church summoned the Italian astronomer, mathematician, and physicist Galileo Galilei to Rome to face charges of heresy for promoting the theory that the earth revolves around the sun. After questioning the seventy-year-old scientist for eighteen days, the tribunal found him guilty and ordered him to confess his errors. In a formal ceremony Galileo abjured, or renounced, his findings. He remained under house arrest until his death in 1642.

FREE SPEECH AND SOCIAL PROGRESS

Those who advocated unconventional ideas displayed a great deal of courage, but their actions did not constitute a coherent social movement, let alone a free speech movement. These defiant speakers were more dedicated to the beliefs they espoused than they were to any right to advocate them. The trial of Galileo, however, sparked interest in free speech as a social good. Coming in the midst of the Renaissance, when European scholars were rediscovering the achievements of the Greek and Roman civilizations, the persecution of a scientist for advancing what appeared to be sound ideas struck many as small-minded and oppressive. Growing confidence in the ability of scholars to distinguish truth from falsehood led the English poet John Milton to argue that ideas should be allowed to compete freely. Responding to the enactment of the Licensing Order by Parliament in 1643, which required publishers to obtain governmental permission before printing any work, Milton argued that prior restraints stifled the kind of discussion that was vital to progress. Milton urged Parliament to adopt the Greek model of open debate. Instead of suppressing books before they were published, he argued, Parliament should allow all authors to place their ideas before the public. If their ideas are false, he reasoned, society will reject them. "Let [Truth] and Falsehood grapple," he wrote. "Who ever knew Truth put to the worse, in a free and open encounter? Her confuting is the best and surest suppressing."[6]

Milton's appeal to Parliament, published under the title *Areopagitica*, marks a turning point in history. Milton's hypothesis that truth could be counted on to curb falsehood offered an attractive alternative to governmental regulation of speech and the press. The removal of prior restraints would not lead to social ills, Milton reasoned, because free speech would regulate itself. This idea launched the modern movement centered around the ideal of free speech, and free speech remains the movement's guiding principle. As syndicated columnist Donald Kaul puts it: "We [free speech] zealots believe that a free society demands a free marketplace of ideas where the good can compete against the bad and the ugly and that, given such a marketplace, the good will win out."[7]

Elegant as Milton's arguments were, they did not persuade Parliament to repeal the Licensing Order. The British legislators renewed the order in 1647, 1648, and 1649. The order lapsed for a period of fifteen months between 1651 and 1653, but Parliament reinstated it in 1653. The order remained in effect in England for another forty-two years until Parliament finally allowed it to expire. The removal of prior restraints in 1695 did not mean the British press was immune from all limits, however. Publishers still could be held accountable for any damage their books, pamphlets, and newspapers might cause after publication. As the British jurist Sir William Blackstone put it, "The liberty of the press is indeed essential to the nature of a free state; but this consists in laying no previous restraints upon publications, and not in freedom from censure for criminal matter when published."[8]

Parliament also took steps to promote free speech. Adopted in 1689, the English Bill of Rights stated, "That the freedom of speech and debates or proceedings in Parliament ought not to be impeached or questioned in any court or place out of Parliament."[9] While these guarantees did not apply to ordinary citizens, they marked an important milestone in the movement because they identified free speech as a fundamental right. The

English Bill of Rights later served as a model for the bill of rights in the English colonies of North America.

CONSTITUTIONAL QUESTIONS IN EARLY AMERICA

In 1776 the American colonists declared their independence from Britain, vowing to throw off the monarchy and replace it with a democratic system of government. After the colonies won their independence from Britain in 1783, the leaders of the Revolution drafted a constitution that called for elections of public officials. To promote the kind of public discussion needed for informed self-rule, many of the founders believed that the constitution should guarantee the right of free speech to all citizens. As James Madison, a member of Congress and future president of the United States, put it: "A popular government, without popular information or the means of acquiring it, is but a Prologue to a Farce or a Tragedy; or, perhaps, both. Knowledge will forever govern ignorance: And a people who mean to be their own Governors, must arm themselves with the power which knowledge gives."[10]

After the Constitution was ratified, some leaders called on Congress to adopt a bill of rights similar to the English Bill of Rights. "A bill of rights is what the people are entitled to against every government on earth, general or particular, and what no just government should refuse or rest on inference,"[11] wrote Thomas Jefferson, author of the Declaration of Independence and future president of the United States. Other leaders, such as Alexander Hamilton, disagreed. Such protections were not necessary, Hamilton argued, because the Constitution did not give the government the power to deprive people of their rights. "Why declare that things shall not be done which there is no power to do?" asked Alexander Hamilton in *The Federalist Papers*, no. 84. "Why, for instance, should it be said that the liberty of the press shall not be restrained, when no power is given by which restrictions may be imposed?"[12]

Those who campaigned for a bill of rights prevailed, and James Madison volunteered to draft the amendments to the

Constitution that would enshrine basic liberties. One of these amendments guaranteed freedom of expression. "The people shall not be deprived or abridged of their right to speak, to write, or to publish their sentiments; and the freedom of the press, as one of the great bulwarks of liberty, shall be inviolable,"[13] Madison wrote in a draft he presented to the House of Representatives on June 8, 1789. A special House committee revised Madison's wording, as did the Senate. The final version of the First Amendment stated simply, "Congress shall make no law . . . abridging freedom of speech, or of the press."[14] On December 15, 1791, Virginia became the eleventh state to ratify the Bill of Rights, making it part of the Constitution. The right to free speech, which had flowered in ancient Greece only to lay dormant under a blanket of tyranny for two thousand years, blossomed once more on American soil.

INTERPRETING THE FIRST AMENDMENT

If constitutions were self-defining and self-enforcing, the struggle for free speech might have ended with the ratification of the First Amendment in 1791. This is not the case, however. Constitutions must be enforced, and to be enforced they must be interpreted by human beings with all their flaws, limitations, and differences—a process awash in vagaries. Unlike Milton's hypothetical model, the real marketplace of ideas rarely offers stark choices between truth and falsehood. More often it features competition between many truths, many falsehoods, or some combination of both. In such an environment, consensus is nearly impossible. This has been true even about the right to free speech itself. As soon as the First Amendment was adopted, people began to debate its meaning.

Most of the founders believed that the First Amendment prohibited only the federal government from restraining speech, not the states. At the time the First Amendment was ratified, the constitutions of Pennsylvania and Delaware contained limits on expression. A year after the First Amendment was ratified, the Virginia legislature passed a law declaring that "Every person . . . who shall by writing or advised speaking, endeavor to instigate the people of this commonwealth to erect or establish such government without such assent as aforesaid, shall be adjudged guilty of a high crime and misdemeanor."[15] Thomas Jefferson reflected the thinking of most when he wrote in a letter to Abigail Adams, "While we deny that Congress have a right to control the freedom of the press, we have ever asserted the right of the states, and their exclusive right, to do so."[16]

The Sedition Act of 1798 provides a vivid example of how intelligent and well-informed people can hold vastly different opinions about free speech and the meaning of the First Amendment. Under threat of war with France, President John Adams, an architect of the American Revolution and the author of the Massachusetts constitution, urged Congress to pass legislation designed to protect the new government from violent overthrow. Congress complied, passing the Sedition Act of July 14, 1798. One section of the Sedition Act made it a criminal offense to "counsel, advise or attempt to procure any insurrection, riot, unlawful assembly, or combination." Another section called for the punishment of any person who would "write, print, utter or publish . . . any false, scandalous and malicious writing or writings against the government of the United States."[17] A report prepared by a committee headed by James Madison maintained that the Sedition Act violated the First Amendment, but the majority of Congress rejected this interpretation. As Supreme Court justice Felix Frankfurter later noted, "In reply it was urged that power to restrict seditious writing was implicit in the acknowledged power of the Federal Government to prohibit seditious acts, and that the liberty of the press did not extend to the sort of speech restricted by the Act."[18]

Under the Sedition Act, twenty-five people, including several newspaper editors, were arrested; ten were convicted. Champions of free speech were outraged. George Hay, a Virginia legislator who served as a U.S. attorney and on the federal bench, savaged the act. He argued that the wording of the First Amendment is self-evident: "The word 'freedom' has meaning.

It is either absolute, that is, exempt from all law, or it is qualified, that is, regulated by law. . . . If it is to be regulated by law, the Amendment that declared that Congress shall make no law to abridge the freedom of the press . . . is the grossest absurdity that ever was conceived by the human mind."[19] The Sedition Act remained in force until it expired in 1801, but the controversy it provoked helped make free speech a national issue.

Restraining Speech in Wartime

Like John Adams before him, Abraham Lincoln feared the power of speech to incite insurrection. Aware of the role the press had played in promoting the secession of the Southern states, Lincoln issued a proclamation after the outbreak of the Civil War that called for the arrest of anyone engaging in "any disloyal practice, affording aid and comfort to Rebels."[20] In Ohio, General Ambrose Burnside, acting on Lincoln's proclamation, had Congressman Clement L. Vallandigham arrested for speaking out against Lincoln and the war. Found guilty by a military court, Vallandigham was banished to the South. Although Vallandigham was not a sympathetic figure in the North, his arrest and conviction raised concern even among Lincoln's supporters that the right to free speech was under siege. The controversy over Vallandigham proved that even in time of national emergency the free speech movement remained alive.

Differences over the ability of the government to restrain speech in wartime surfaced again during World War I. Convicted of violating the Espionage Act of 1917 by encouraging young men to resist the draft, Charles T. Schenck and Elizabeth Baer appealed their convictions to the U.S. Supreme Court. In the first free speech case to reach the high court, the justices ruled unanimously that the First Amendment did not prevent the government from punishing speech that incited lawless action. The decision in *Schenck v. United States* (1919) made it clear that the right to free expression has limits. However, it also suggested that laws restraining speech must be narrowly tailored to serve compelling interests of the government.

EXTENDING FREE SPEECH DEFINITIONS

Encouraged by the willingness of the high court to apply rigorous constitutional tests to the Espionage Act, free speech advocates realized that they could use the courts to test the constitutionality of other restraints on speech. The first and most successful organization to pursue this strategy was the American Civil Liberties Union (ACLU). In its first case before the U.S. Supreme Court, the ACLU sought to overturn the conviction of Benjamin Gitlow for violating the 1902 criminal anarchy law of New York by publishing a pamphlet entitled *The Left-Wing Manifesto*. The high court upheld Gitlow's conviction, but in a landmark interpretation it accepted the ACLU's argument that the First Amendment applied not only to federal laws but to state laws as well. "For present purposes we may and do assume that freedom of speech and of the press—which are protected by the First Amendment from abridgment by Congress—are among the fundamental personal rights and 'liberties' protected by the due process clause of the Fourteenth Amendment from impairment by the States,"[21] wrote Justice Edward T. Sanford. By extending the guarantees of free speech and a free press to the states, the high court invigorated the free speech movement.

Ever since *Gitlow v. People of the State of New York* (1925), the ACLU and other members of the free speech movement have continued to challenge the constitutionality of laws, injunctions, and executive orders restricting expression. Through these efforts, free speech advocates won a number of important victories, including the right to burn the American flag in protest, the right to wear an armband in school as a sign of protest, the right of an individual to possess pornography, and the right to advocate the overthrow of the government. In one landmark case, *New York Times Co. v. United States* (1971), a coalition of free speech advocates convinced the U.S. Supreme Court to vacate an injunction that prevented the *New York Times* from publishing secret documents relating to the Vietnam War. In another important case, *Reno v. American Civil Liberties Union* (1997), the ACLU led a successful fight to invalidate the Communications

Decency Act (CDA), which banned indecent and patently offensive material on the Internet.

A DIFFERENT KIND OF MOVEMENT

The decision to pursue judicial rather than legislative remedies makes the continuous fight for free speech somewhat unique among American social movements. Most movements, such as the abolitionist movement and the woman suffrage movement, have tried to effect change by petitioning Congress or the states to enact legislation or amend the Constitution. With the Constitution already guaranteeing free expression, leaders of the free speech movement have focused their efforts on persuading the judiciary to broaden the scope of the First Amendment. This strategy provides free speech advocates with a simple and economical method to expand the right of free speech. Rather than having to petition legislatures state by state and even city by city to repeal certain kinds of laws that limit expression, free speech advocates instead can have all such laws struck down by a single Supreme Court decision.

Ignoring the legislative process has its drawbacks, however. Since laws enacted by the legislatures reflect the will of the people, efforts to overturn laws rather than repeal them strikes many people as undemocratic. Critics of the free speech movement argue that its leaders substitute their own judgment for the judgment of the people, thwarting democracy. By turning their backs on the public debate and refusing to put their beliefs to the test in the marketplace of ideas, the leaders of the ongoing struggle for unfettered free speech appear to lack confidence in the fundamental principle that underlies their movement. Critics see them as hypocrites, unwilling to live by the principles they espouse.

Members of the free speech movement remain unconcerned by such charges. They believe their cause to be a noble one in part because it is fundamentally unpopular. They see dangers in permitting the majority to dictate what words and images will be allowed to circulate freely, and they fiercely resist such majoritarianism. They stand by the words of British philosopher

John Stuart Mill, who wrote, "Society has no more right to tell the individual what to think than the individual would have in telling the majority what to think, if he could do so."[22] Defenders of unrestrained free speech continue to fight for the freedom to express all ideas, no matter how unpopular some might be.

NOTES

1. L.W. King, trans., "Hammurabi's Code of Laws," *Readings from the Ancient Near East*, University of Evansville, Illinois, http://eawc.evansville.edu/anthology/hammurabi.htm.

2. Exodus 23:1 (New International Version).

3. Euripides, *The Complete Greek Drama,* vol. 1, eds. Whitney J. Oates and Eugene O'Neill Jr., trans. E.P. Coleridge. New York: Random House, 1938, pp. 331–32.

4. Quoted in Hayden Pellicia, ed., *Selected Dialogues of Plato,* trans. Benjamin Jowett. New York: Modern Library, 2000, p. 302.

5. Quoted in Pellicia, *Selected Dialogues of Plato,* p. 301.

6. John Milton, *Areopagitica.* London: J.M. Dent, 1955, p. 36.

7. Donald Kaul, "Media Violence May Wound Us, but Censorship Cuts Deeper," *Liberal Opinion Week*, March 28, 1994, p. 5.

8. Quoted in J.W. Erlich, ed., *Erlich's Blackstone.* San Carlos, CA: Nourse, 1959, p. 813.

9. Avalon Project at Yale Law School, "The English Bill of Rights," www.yale.edu/lawweb/avalon/england.htm.

10. Quoted in Karl Tage Olson, "The Constitutionality of Department of Defense Press Restrictions on Wartime Correspondence Covering the Persian Gulf War," *Drake Law Review*, 1992, p. 512.

11. Quoted in Digital History, "Online History Textbook," www.digitalhistory.uh.edu/database/article_display.cfm?HHID=295.

12. Alexander Hamilton, *The Federalist Papers,* no. 84, Avalon Project at Yale Law School, www.yale.edu/lawweb/Avalon/federal/fed84.htm.

13. Quoted in FindLaw Internet Legal Resources, "Freedom of Expression—Speech and Press, Adoption and the Common Law Background," http://caselaw.findlaw.com/data/constitution/amendment01/06.html.

14. U.S. Constitution, First Amendment.

15. Va. Code, 1803, c. CXXXVI.

16. Quoted in *Dennis v. United States,* 341 U.S. 494 (1951).

17. Avalon Project at Yale Law School, "An Act for the Punishment of Certain Crimes Against the United States," Sections 1 and 2, www.yale.edu/lawweb/Avalon/statutes/sedact.htm.

18. *Dennis v. United States.*

19. George Hay, *Two Essays on the Liberty of the Press.* New York: De Capo, 1970, p. 24.

20. Quoted in Michael Kent Curtis, *Free Speech, "The People's Darling Privilege": Struggles for Freedom of Expression in American History.* Durham, NC: Duke University Press, 2000, p. 306.

21. *Gitlow v. People of the State of New York,* 268 U.S. 652 (1925).

22. John Stuart Mill, *The Basic Writings of John Stuart Mill: On Liberty, the Subjection of Women and Utilitarianism.* New York: Modern Library, 2002, p. 18.

CHAPTER 1

PHILOSOPHICAL ORIGINS

AMERICAN
SOCIAL
MOVEMENTS

Speech Is Self-Regulating

JOHN MILTON

The author of *Paradise Lost*, John Milton is considered by many to be the second-greatest English poet, after Shakespeare. Born into a prosperous London family in 1608, Milton received a private education as a boy then enrolled in St. Paul's School, Cambridge, in 1625. He continued his studies at Christ's College, receiving a master of arts degree in 1632. Milton had planned to become a minister, but he became dissatisfied with the Church of England and decided to pursue literature instead. In 1638 Milton traveled to Italy to study. While on the continent, Milton met several notable figures, including the scientist Galileo and the legal scholar Grotius. After returning to England, Milton wrote several pamphlets supporting reforms to the Church of England. He also took issue with an act passed by the British Parliament in 1643 calling for "the Regulation of Printing, and for suppressing the great late abuses and frequent disorders in Printing." In a pamphlet addressed to Parliament entitled *Aeropagitica*, excerpted below, Milton called for an end to prior restraint of the press. Such limits were unnecessary, Milton argued, because good ideas could be counted on to suppress bad ideas before they caused any harm. Under Milton's scheme, the role of the government is not to suppress speech it deems undesirable, but to create an environment in which ideas—good and bad alike—can compete freely.

Milton's hypothesis that speech could regulate itself was ignored in its day but has been embraced by generations of free speech advocates and acknowledged by many courts. In *Dennis v. United States*, U.S. Supreme Court chief justice Frederick M. Vinson stated that the First Amendment of the U.S. Constitution, which guarantees

John Milton, *The Portable Milton*. New York: Viking Press, 1967.

the right to free speech, is founded on the notion that good ideas will triumph over bad ideas: "The basis of the First Amendment is the hypothesis that speech can rebut speech, propaganda will answer propaganda, free debate of ideas will result in the wisest governmental policies. It is for this reason that this Court has recognized the inherent value of free discourse."

I deny not but that it is of greatest concernment in the church and commonwealth to have a vigilant eye how books demean themselves, as well as men, and thereafter to confine, imprison, and do sharpest justice on them as malefactors. For books are not absolutely dead things, but do contain a potency of life in them to be as active as that soul was whose progeny they are; nay, they do preserve as in a vial the purest efficacy and extraction of that living intellect that bred them. I know they are as lively, and as vigorously productive, as those fabulous dragon's teeth; and being sown up and down, may chance to spring up armed men. And yet, on the other hand, unless wariness be used, as good almost kill a man as kill a good book: who kills a man kills a reasonable creature, God's image; but he who destroys a good book, kills reason itself, kills the image of God, as it were, in the eye. Many a man lives a burden to the earth; but a good book is the precious life-blood of a master spirit, embalmed and treasured up on purpose to a life beyond life. . . . We should be wary, therefore, what persecution we raise against the living labors of public men, how we spill that seasoned life of man preserved and stored up in books; since we see a kind of homicide may be thus committed, sometimes a martyrdom; and if it extend to the whole impression, a kind of massacre, whereof the execution ends not in the slaying of an elemental life, but strikes at that ethereal and fifth essence, the breath of reason itself, slays an immortality rather than a life. . . .

THE VALUE OF READING ALL BOOKS
[A bishop of the Roman Catholic Church] Dionysius Alexandrinus was, about the year 240, a person of great name in the

church for piety and learning, who had wont to avail himself much against heretics by being conversant in their books; until a certain presbyter laid it scrupulously to his conscience, how he durst venture himself among those defiling volumes. The worthy man, loth to give offence, fell into a new debate with himself what was to be thought; when suddenly a vision sent from God (it is his own epistle that so avers it) confirmed him in these words: "Read any books, whatever come to thy hands, for thou art sufficient both to judge aright and to examine each matter." To this revelation he assented the sooner, as he confesses, because it was answerable to that of the Apostle to the Thessalonians: "Prove all things, hold fast that which is good." And he might have added another remarkable saying of the same author: "To the pure, all things are pure"; not only meats and drinks, but all kind of knowledge, whether of good or evil: the knowledge cannot defile, nor consequently the books, if the will and conscience be not defiled. For books are as meats and viands are, some of good, some of evil substance....

I conceive, therefore, that when God did enlarge the universal diet of man's body, saving ever the rules of temperance, he then also, as before, left arbitrary the dieting and repasting of our minds; as wherein every mature man might have to exercise his own leading capacity....

THE KNOWLEDGE OF GOOD AND EVIL

Good and evil we know in the field of this world grow up together almost inseparably; and the knowledge of good is so involved and interwoven with the knowledge of evil, and in so many cunning resemblances hardly to be discerned, that those confused seeds which were imposed on Psyche as an incessant labor to cull out and sort asunder, were not more intermixed. It was from out the rind of one apple tasted that the knowledge of good and evil, as two twins cleaving together, leaped forth into the world.... As therefore the state of man now is, what wisdom can there be to choose, what continence to forbear, without the knowledge of evil? ... I cannot praise a fugitive and cloistered virtue, unexercised and unbreathed, that never sallies out and sees her adversary, but slinks out of the race where that immortal garland is to be run for, not without dust and heat. Assuredly we bring not innocence into the world, we bring impurity much rather; that which purifies us is trial, and trial is by what is contrary. . . . Since therefore the knowledge and survey of vice is in this world so necessary to the constituting of human virtue, and the scanning of error to the confirmation of truth, how can we more safely, and with less danger, scout into the regions of sin and falsity than by reading all manner of tractates and hearing all manner of reason? And this is the benefit which may be had of books promiscuously read. . . .

Books are not temptations nor vanities, but useful drugs and materials wherewith to temper and compose effective and strong medicines, which man's life cannot want. . . . See the ingenuity of truth, who, when she gets a free and willing hand, opens herself faster than the pace of method and discourse can overtake her. . . .

Suppose we could expel sin by [banishing all sinful things]: look how much we thus expel of sin, so much we expel of virtue, for the matter of them both is the same; remove that, and ye remove them both alike. This justifies the high providence of God, who, though he command us temperance, justice, continence, yet pours out before us even to a profuseness all desirable things, and gives us minds that can wander beyond all limit and satiety. Why should we then affect a rigor contrary to the manner of God and of nature, by abridging or scanting those means, which books freely permitted are, both to the trial of virtue and the exercise of truth? . . .

CENSORSHIP IS DEMEANING

What advantage is it to be a man over it is to be a boy at school, if we have only scaped the ferula [a cane used to punish children] to come under the fescue [a rod used in pointing out letters in teaching children to read] of an Imprimatur [license to print a book]; if serious and elaborate writings, as if they were no more than the theme of a grammar-lad under his pedagogue, must not be uttered without the cursory eyes of a temporizing and extemporizing licenser? He who is not trusted with his own actions, his drift not being known to be evil, and standing to the hazard of law and penalty, has no great argument to think himself reputed, in the commonwealth wherein he was born, for other than a fool or a foreigner....

And how can a man teach with authority, which is the life of teaching, how can he be a doctor in his book, as he ought to be, or else had better be silent, whenas all he teaches, all he delivers, is but under the tuition, under the correction, of his patriarchal licenser, to blot or alter what precisely accords not with the hidebound humor which he calls his judgment? When every acute reader, upon the first sight of a pedantic license, will be ready with these like words to ding the book a quoit's distance from him: "I hate a pupil teacher, I endure not an instructor that comes to me under the wardship of an overseeing fist. I know nothing of the licenser, but that I have his own hand here for his arrogance; who shall warrant me his judgment?" "The state, sir," replies the stationer, but has a quick return: "The state shall be my governors, but not my critics; they may be mistaken in the choice of a licenser, as easily as this licenser may be mistaken in an author. This is some common stuff."...

And as it is a particular disesteem of every knowing person alive, and most injurious to the written labors and monuments of the dead, so to me it seems an undervaluing and vilifying of the whole nation. I cannot set so light by all the invention, the art, the wit, the grave and solid judgment which is in England, as that it can be comprehended in any twenty capacities, how good so-ever; much less that it should not pass except their superintendence be over it, except it be sifted and strained with their strainers, that it should be uncurrent without their manual stamp. Truth and understanding are not such wares as to be monopolized and traded in by tickets and statutes and standards. We must not think to make a staple commodity of all the knowledge in the land, to mark and license it like our broadcloth and our woolpacks....

Well knows he who uses to consider, that our faith and knowledge thrives by exercise, as well as our limbs and complexion. Truth is compared in Scripture to a streaming fountain; if her waters flow not in a perpetual progression, they sicken into a muddy pool of conformity and tradition. A man may be a heretic in the truth; and if he believe things only because his pastor says so, or the Assembly so determines, without knowing other reason, though his belief be true, yet the very truth he holds becomes his heresy. . . .

Give me the liberty to know, to utter, and to argue freely according to conscience, above all liberties. . . .

And now the time in special is, by privilege to write and speak what may help to the further discussing of matters in agitation. . . . And though all the winds of doctrine were let loose to play upon the earth, so truth be in the field, we do injuriously by licensing and prohibiting to misdoubt her strength. Let her and falsehood grapple; who ever knew truth put to the worse, in a free and open encounter? Her confuting is the best and surest suppressing. . . .

For who knows not that truth is strong, next to the Almighty? She needs no policies, nor stratagems, nor licensings to make her victorious; those are the shifts and the defences that error uses against her power. . . .

If it come to prohibiting, there is not aught more likely to be prohibited than truth itself, whose first appearance, to our eyes bleared and dimmed with prejudice and custom, is more unsightly and unplausible than many errors, even as the person is of many a great man slight and contemptible to see to? . . .

This I know, that errors in a good government and in a bad are equally almost incident; for what magistrate may not be misinformed, and much the sooner, if liberty of printing be reduced into the power of a few? But to redress willingly and speedily what hath been erred, and in highest authority to esteem a plain advertisement more than others have done a sumptuous bribe, is a virtue, honored Lords and Commons, answerable to your highest actions, and whereof none can participate but greatest and wisest men.

The Rights of Individuals

WILLIAM BLACKSTONE

Sir William Blackstone was born in London in 1723. The son of a silk merchant, Blackstone received his early education at Charterhouse then enrolled in Pembroke College in Oxford. After graduation, he studied law at Middle Temple College and Oxford University, earning a doctorate of law degree in 1750. Blackstone became a professor of law at Oxford and in 1758 inaugurated the study of English law—a break from the tradition of studying only Roman law. Eventually, Blackstone collected his lectures and published them as *Commentaries on the Laws of England* (4 vol., 1765–1769)—considered the clearest and most complete treatment of English law ever produced.

Blackstone's *Commentaries* continue to be cited not only by British law schools and courts, but by American ones as well. In this essay, Blackstone describes the rights of the individuals and the protections they receive from the government. He also discusses freedom of expression, arguing against prior restraints of printed works but allowing for the punishment of those who use speech or the press to infringe on the rights of others—a distinction that continues to be drawn by courts today.

As municipal law is a rule of civil conduct, commanding what is right, and prohibiting what is wrong; it follows, that the primary and principal objects of the law are rights and wrongs. I shall in the first place consider the rights that are commanded, and secondly, the wrongs that are forbidden by the laws of England.

Rights are, however, liable to another subdivision: being ei-

William Blackstone, *Ehrlich's Blackstone*, edited by J.W. Ehrlich. San Carlos, CA: Nourse Publishing Company, 1959.

ther, first, those which concern and are annexed to the persons of men; and are then called the rights of persons; or they are secondly, such as a man may acquire over external objects, or things unconnected with his person, which are styled the rights of things. Wrongs also are divisible into, first, private wrongs, which, being in infringement merely of particular rights, concern individuals only, and are called civil injuries; and secondly, public wrongs, which, being a breach of general and public rights, affect the whole community, and are called crimes and misdemeanors. . . .

RIGHTS OF PERSONS

Now the rights of persons that are commanded to be observed by the municipal law are of two sorts: First, such as are due from every citizen, which are usually called civil duties; and secondly, such as belong to him, which is the more popular acceptation of rights. Both may, indeed, be comprised in this latter division; for, as all social duties are of a relative nature, at the same time that they are due from one man, or set of men, they must also be due to another. . . .

The rights of persons considered in their natural capacities are also of two sorts, absolute and relative. Absolute, which are such as appertain and belong to particular men, merely as individuals or single persons: relative, which are incident to them as members of society, and standing in various relations to each other. The first, that is, absolute rights, will be the subject of the present chapter.

ABSOLUTE RIGHTS

By the absolute rights of individuals we mean those which are so in their primary and strictest sense; such as would belong to their persons merely in a state of nature, and which every man is entitled to enjoy, whether out of society or in it. . . .

For the principal aim of society is to protect individuals in the enjoyment of those absolute rights, which were vested in them by the immutable laws of nature; but which could not be preserved in peace without that mutual assistance and intercourse, which is gained by the institution of friendly and social communities. Hence it follows, that the first and primary ends of human laws is to maintain and regulate these absolute rights of individuals.

Such rights as are social and relative result from, and are posterior to, the formation of states and societies; so that to maintain and regulate there is clearly a subsequent consideration. Therefore the principal view of human laws is, or ought always to be, to explain, protect, and enforce such rights as are absolute, which in themselves are few and simple; and, then, such rights as are relative, which arising from a variety of connections, will be far more numerous and more complicated. These will take up a greater space in any code of laws, and hence may appear to be more attended to, though in reality they are not, than the rights of the former kind. Let us therefore proceed to examine how far all laws ought, and how far the laws of England actually do, take notice of these absolute rights, and provide for their lasting security.

NATURAL LIBERTY

The absolute rights of man considered as a free agent, endowed with discernment to know good from evil, and with power of choosing those measures which appear to him to be most desirable, are usually summed up in one general appellation, and denominated the natural liberty of mankind. This natural liberty consists properly in a power of acting as one thinks fit, without any restraint or control, unless by the law of nature; being a right inherent in us by birth, and one of the gifts of God to man at his creation, when he endued him with the faculty of free will.

But every man, when he enters into society, gives up a part of his natural liberty, as the price of so valuable a purchase; and, in consideration of receiving the advantages of mutual commerce, obliges himself to conform to those laws, which the community has thought proper to establish. This species of legal obedience and conformity is infinitely more desirable than that wild and savage liberty which is sacrificed to obtain it.

Civil Liberty

For no man, that considers a moment, would wish to retain the absolute and uncontrolled power of doing whatever he pleases: the consequence of which is, that every other man would also have the same power; and then there would be no security to individuals in any of the enjoyments of life. Political, therefore, or civil, liberty, which is that of a member of society, is no other than natural liberty so far restrained by human laws as is necessary and expedient for the general advantage of the public.

Hence we may collect that the law, which restrains a man from doing mischief to his fellow citizens, though it diminishes the natural, increases the civil liberty of mankind; but that every wanton and causeless restraint of the will of the subject, whether practiced by a monarch, a nobility, or a popular assembly, is a degree of tyranny: nay, that even laws themselves, whether made with or without our consent, if they regulate and constrain our conduct in matters of mere indifference, without any good end in view, are regulations destructive of liberty; whereas if any public advantage can arise from observing such precepts, the control of our private inclinations, in one or two particular points, will conduce to preserve our general freedom in others of more importance; by supporting that state of society which alone can secure our independence; so that laws, when prudently framed, are by no means subversive but rather introductive of liberty; for where there is no law there is no freedom.

But then, that constitution or frame of government, that system of laws, is alone calculated to maintain civil liberty, which leaves the subject entire master of his own conduct, except in those points wherein the public good requires some direction or restraint. . . .

Public Wrongs

We are next to consider offenses against the public peace, the conservation of which is entrusted to the king and his officers. These offenses are either such as are in actual breach of the peace, or constructively so, by tending to make others break it. . . .

Spreading false news, to make discord between the king and nobility, or concerning any great man of the realm, is punished by common law with fine and imprisonment. . . .

False and pretended prophecies, with intent to disturb the peace, are equally unlawful, and more penal; as they raise enthusiastic jealousies in the people, and terrify them with imaginary fears. . . .

Besides actual breaches of the peace, anything that tends to provoke or excite others to break it is an offense of the same denomination. Therefore, challenges to fight, either by word or letter, or to be the bearer of such challenge, are punishable by fine and imprisonment, according to the circumstances of the offense. . . .

Of a nature very similar to challenges are libels, libelli famosi (Defamatory writings), which, taken in their largest and most extensive sense, signify any writings, pictures or the like, or an immoral or illegal tendency; but, in the sense under which we are now to consider them, are malicious defamations of any person, and especially a magistrate, made public by either printing, writing, signs or pictures, in order to provoke him to wrath or expose him to public hatred, contempt and ridicule. The direct tendency of these libels is the breach of the public peace, by stirring up the objects of them to revenge, and perhaps to bloodshed. . . .

LIBERTY OF THE PRESS

In this, and the other instances which we have lately considered, where blasphemous, immoral, treasonable, schismatical, seditious, or scandalous libels are punished by the English law, some with a greater, others with a less, degree of severity, the liberty of the press, properly understood, is by no means infringed or violated. The liberty of the press is indeed essential to the nature of a free state; but this consists in laying no previous restraints upon publications, and not in freedom from censure for criminal matter when published.

Every freeman has an undoubted right to lay what sentiments he pleases before the public: to forbid this is to destroy the freedom of the press, but if he publishes what is improper, mischievous or illegal, he must take the consequence of his own temerity. To subject the press to the restrictive power of a licenser, as was formerly done, both before and since the revolution, is to subject all freedom of sentiment to the prejudices of one man, and make him the arbitrary and infallible judge of all controverted points in learning, religion and government.

But to punish (as the law does at present) any dangerous or offensive writings which, when published, shall on a fair and impartial trial be adjudged of a pernicious tendency, is necessary for the preservation of peace and good order, of government and religion—the only solid foundations of civil liberty. Thus the will of individuals is still left free; the abuse only of that free will is the object of legal punishment.

Neither is any restraint hereby laid upon freedom of thought or inquiry: liberty of private sentiment is still left; the disseminating, or making public, of bad sentiments, destructive to the ends of society, is a crime which society corrects. A man (says a fine writer on this subject) may be allowed to keep poisons in his closet, but not publicly to vend them as cordials. To this we may add, that the only plausible argument heretofore used for restraining the just freedom of the press, "that it was necessary, to prevent the daily abuse of it," will entirely lose its force when it is shown (by a seasonable exertion of the laws) that the press cannot be abused to any bad purpose without incurring a suitable punishment; where it never can be used to any good one, when under the control of an inspector. So true will it be found, that to censure the licentiousness, is to maintain the liberty, of the press.

Social Liberty

JOHN STUART MILL

The eldest son of author and philosopher James Mill, John Stuart
Mill was born in London in 1806. As a child, Mill was educated at
home by his father with help from Jeremy Bentham, the originator
of utilitarian philosophy. In 1823 Mill became a clerk for the East
India company. Over the next thirty-six years, Mill rose through the
company ranks to become the head of the examiner's office. He followed his father into the realm of philosophy, publishing *A System
of Logic* (1843) and *Principles of Political Economy* (1848). In 1851 Mill
married Harriet Taylor, who shared his interest in philosophy. Together they worked on the book *On Liberty* that appeared in 1859.
Mill published *Utilitarianism* in 1863 and *Auguste Comte and Positivism*
in 1865. He served as a member of Parliament from 1865 to 1868.
After he retired, he worked on his *Autobiography*, which was published in 1873, the year of his death.

In this essay from *On Liberty*, Mill describes individual liberty as
an absolute right that must be protected not only from interference
by the government but also from coercion by public opinion. His
defense of the individual against "the tyranny of the majority" is a
cornerstone of modern free speech philosophy.

The subject of this Essay is not the so-called Liberty of the
Will, but Civil, or Social Liberty: the nature and limits of
the power which can be legitimately exercised by society over
the individual. A question seldom stated, and hardly ever discussed, in general terms, but which profoundly influences the
practical controversies of the age by its latent presence, and is
likely soon to make itself recognized as the vital question of the
future. It is so far from being new, that, in a certain sense, it has
divided mankind, almost from the remotest ages; but in the

John Stuart Mill, *On Liberty*, 1859.

stage of progress into which the more civilized portions of the species have now entered, it presents itself under new conditions, and requires a different and more fundamental treatment.

Protection Against Tyranny

The struggle between Liberty and Authority is the most conspicuous feature in the portions of history with which we are earliest familiar, particularly in that of Greece, Rome, and England. But in old times this contest was between subjects, or some classes of subjects, and the government. By liberty, was meant protection against the tyranny of the political rulers. The rulers were conceived (except in some of the popular governments of Greece) as in a necessarily antagonistic position to the people whom they ruled. . . . The aim . . . of patriots, was to set limits to the power which the ruler should be suffered to exercise over the community; and this limitation was what they meant by liberty. It was attempted in two ways. First, by obtaining a recognition of certain immunities, called political liberties or rights, which it was to be regarded as a breach of duty in the ruler to infringe, and which, if he did infringe, specific resistance, or general rebellion, was held to be justifiable. A second, and generally a later expedient, was the establishment of constitutional checks; by which the consent of the community, or of a body of some sort supposed to represent its interests, was made a necessary condition to some of the more important acts of the governing power. . . .

Tyranny of the Majority

In time, . . . a democratic republic came to occupy a large portion of the earth's surface, and made itself felt as one of the most powerful members of the community of nations; and elective and responsible government became subject to the observations and criticisms which wait upon a great existing fact. It was now perceived that such phrases as "self-government," and "the power of the people over themselves," do not express the true state of the case. The "people" who exercise the power, are not always the same people with those over whom it is exercised; and the "self-government" spoken of, is not the government of each by himself, but of each by all the rest. The will of the people, moreover, practically means, the will of the most numerous or the most active *part* of the people; the majority, or those who succeed in making themselves accepted as the majority: the people, consequently, *may* desire to oppress a part of their number; and precautions are as much needed against this, as against any other abuse of power. The limitation, therefore, of the power of government over individuals, loses none of its importance when the holders of power are regularly accountable to the community, that is, to the strongest party therein. This view of things, recommending itself equally to the intelligence of thinkers and to the inclination of those important classes in European society to whose real or supposed interests democracy is adverse, has had no difficulty in establishing itself, and in political speculations "the tyranny of the majority" is now generally included among the evils against which society requires to be on its guard.

SOCIAL TYRANNY

Like other tyrannies, the tyranny of the majority was at first, and is still vulgarly, held in dread, chiefly as operating through the acts of the public authorities. But reflecting persons perceived that when society is itself the tyrant—society collectively, over the separate individuals who compose it—its means of tyrannizing are not restricted to the acts which it may do by the hands of its political functionaries. Society can and does execute its own mandates: and if it issues wrong mandates instead of right, or any mandates at all in things with which it ought not to meddle, it practises a social tyranny more formidable than many kinds of political oppression, since, though not usually upheld by such extreme penalties, it leaves fewer means of escape, penetrating much more deeply into the details of life, and enslaving the soul itself. Protection, therefore, against the tyranny of the magistrate is not enough; there needs protection also against the tyranny of the prevailing opinion and feeling; against the tendency of society to impose, by other means than civil penalties, its own ideas and practices as rules of conduct on those who dissent from them; to fetter the development, and, if possible, prevent the formation, of any individuality not in harmony with its ways, and compel all characters to fashion themselves upon the model of its own. There is a limit to the legitimate interference of collective opinion with individual independence; and to find that limit, and maintain it against encroachment, is as indispensable to a good condition of human affairs, as protection against political despotism. . . .

The likings and dislikings of society, or of some powerful portion of it, are . . . the main thing which has practically determined the rules laid down for general observance, under the penalties of law or opinion. And in general, those who have been in advance of society in thought and feeling, have left this condition of things unassailed in principle, however they may have come into conflict with it in some of its details. They have occupied themselves rather in inquiring what things society ought to like or dislike, than in questioning whether its likings or dislikings should be a law to individuals. . . .

LIMITS OF LIBERTY

The object of this Essay is to assert one very simple principle, as entitled to govern absolutely the dealings of society with the individual in the way of compulsion and control, whether the means used be physical force in the form of legal penalties, or the moral coercion of public opinion. That principle is, that the sole end for which mankind are warranted, individually or collectively, in interfering with the liberty of action of any of their number, is self-protection. That the only purpose for which power can be rightfully exercised over any member of a civilized community, against his will, is to prevent harm to others. His own good, either physical or moral, is not a sufficient warrant. He cannot rightfully be compelled to do or forbear because it will be better for him to do so, because it will make him happier, because, in the opinions of others, to do so would be wise, or even right. These are good reasons for remonstrating with him, or reasoning with him, or persuading him, or entreating him, but not for compelling him, or visiting him with any evil, in case he do otherwise. To justify that, the conduct from which it is desired to deter him must be calculated to produce evil to some one else. The only part of the conduct of any one, for which he is amenable to society, is that which concerns others. In the part which merely concerns himself, his independence is, of right, absolute. Over himself, over his own body and mind, the individual is sovereign. . . .

If any one does an act hurtful to others, there is a *primâ facie* case for punishing him, by law, or, where legal penalties are not safely applicable, by general disapprobation. There are also many positive acts for the benefit of others, which he may rightfully be compelled to perform; such as, to give evidence in a court of justice; to bear his fair share in the common defence, or in any other joint work necessary to the interest of the society of which he enjoys the protection; and to perform certain acts of individual beneficence, such as saving a fellow creature's life, or interposing to protect the defenceless against ill-usage, things which whenever it is obviously a man's duty to do, he may rightfully be made responsible to society for not doing. A person may cause evil to others not only by his actions but by his inaction, and in either case he is justly accountable to them for the injury. . . .

FREEDOM OF THOUGHT AND OPINION

But there is a sphere of action in which society, as distinguished from the individual, has, if any, only an indirect interest; comprehending all that portion of a person's life and conduct which affects only himself, or, if it also affects others, only with their free, voluntary, and undeceived consent and participation. . . . This, then, is the appropriate region of human liberty. It comprises, first, the inward domain of consciousness; demanding liberty of conscience, in the most comprehensive sense; liberty of thought and feeling; absolute freedom of opinion and sentiment on all subjects, practical or speculative, scientific, moral, or theological. The liberty of expressing and publishing opinions may seem to fall under a different principle, since it belongs to that part of the conduct of an individual which concerns other people; but, being almost of as much importance as the liberty of thought itself, and resting in great part on the same reasons, is practically inseparable from it. Secondly, the principle requires liberty of tastes and pursuits; of framing the plan of our life to suit our own character; of doing as we like, subject to such consequences as may follow; without impediment from our fellow-creatures, so long as what we do does not harm them, even though they should think our conduct foolish, perverse, or wrong. Thirdly, from this liberty of each individual, follows the liberty, within the same limits, of combination among individuals; freedom to unite, for any purpose not involving harm to others: the persons combining being supposed to be of full age, and not forced or deceived.

No society in which these liberties are not, on the whole, respected, is free, whatever may be its form of government; and none is completely free in which they do not exist absolute and unqualified. The only freedom which deserves the name, is that of pursuing our own good in our own way, so long as we do not attempt to deprive others of theirs, or impede their efforts to obtain it. Each is the proper guardian of his own health, whether bodily, or mental and spiritual. Mankind are greater gainers by suffering each other to live as seems good to themselves, than by compelling each to live as seems good to the rest.

Though this doctrine is anything but new, and, to some persons, may have the air of a truism, there is no doctrine which stands more directly opposed to the general tendency of existing opinion and practice. Society has expended fully as much effort in the attempt (according to its lights) to compel people to conform to its notions of personal, as of social excellence. . . .

There is . . . in the world at large an increasing inclination to stretch unduly the powers of society over the individual, both by the force of opinion and even by that of legislation: and as the tendency of all the changes taking place in the world is to strengthen society, and diminish the power of the individual, this encroachment is not one of the evils which tend spontaneously to disappear, but, on the contrary, to grow more and more formidable. The disposition of mankind, whether as rulers or as fellow-citizens, to impose their own opinions and inclinations as a rule of conduct on others, is so energetically supported by some of the best and by some of the worst feelings incident to human nature, that it is hardly ever kept under restraint by anything but want of power; and as the power is not declining, but growing, unless a strong barrier of moral conviction can be raised against the mischief, we must expect, in the present circumstances of the world, to see it increase.

It will be convenient for the argument, if, instead of at once entering upon the general thesis, we confine ourselves in the first instance to a single branch of it, on which the principle here stated is, if not fully, yet to a certain point, recognized by the current opinions. This one branch is the Liberty of Thought: from which it is impossible to separate the cognate liberty of speaking and of writing. Although these liberties, to some considerable amount, form part of the political morality of all countries which profess religious toleration and free institutions, the grounds, both philosophical and practical, on which they rest, are perhaps not so familiar to the general mind, nor so thoroughly appreciated by many even of the leaders of opinion, as might have been expected. Those grounds, when rightly understood, are of much wider application than to only one division of the subject, and a thorough consideration of this part of the question will be found the best introduction to the remainder. . . .

LIBERTY OF THE PRESS

The time, it is to be hoped, is gone by, when any defence would be necessary of the "liberty of the press" as one of the securities against corrupt or tyrannical government. No argument, we may suppose, can now be needed, against permitting a legislature or an executive, not identified in interest with the people, to prescribe opinions to them, and determine what doctrines or what arguments they shall be allowed to hear. This aspect of the question, besides, has been so often and so triumphantly enforced by preceding writers, that it needs not be specially insisted on in this place. . . .

Speaking generally, it is not, in constitutional countries, to be apprehended, that the government, whether completely responsible to the people or not, will often attempt to control the expression of opinion, except when in doing so it makes itself the organ of the general intolerance of the public. Let us suppose, therefore, that the government is entirely at one with the people, and never thinks of exerting any power of coercion unless in agreement with what it conceives to be their voice. But I deny the right of the people to exercise such coercion, either by themselves or by their government. The power itself is illegitimate. The best government has no more title to it than the worst. It is as noxious, or more noxious, when exerted in accordance with public opinion, than when in opposition to it. If all mankind minus one, were of one opinion, and only one person were of the contrary opinion, mankind would be no more justified in silencing that one person, than he, if he had the power, would be justified in silencing mankind. Were an opinion a personal possession of no value except to the owner; if to be obstructed in the enjoyment of it were simply a private injury, it would make some difference whether the injury was inflicted only on a few persons or on many. But the peculiar evil of silencing the expression of an opinion is, that it is robbing the human race; posterity as well as the existing generation; those who dissent from the opinion, still more than those who hold it. If the opinion is right, they are deprived of the opportunity of exchanging error for truth: if wrong, they lose, what is almost as great a benefit, the clearer perception and livelier impression of truth, produced by its collision with error.

CHAPTER 2

THE FIRST AMENDMENT AND CONSTITUTIONAL FREE SPEECH

AMERICAN
SOCIAL
MOVEMENTS

The Limits of Free Speech

JOSEPH STORY

Joseph Story was born in Marblehead, Massachusetts, in 1779, at the height of the Revolutionary War. His father, a physician, served under General George Washington during the campaign in New Jersey. As a youngster, Story developed a lifelong interest in poetry and began writing verses before he was twelve. Story hoped to achieve fame as a writer, but after graduating from Harvard College he decided to study law. In 1801 Story passed the bar exam and established a practice in Salem. In 1804 he published a fifteen hundred–line poem, *The Power of Solitude*, but, embarrassed by its poor reception, bought up copies of the book and burned them.

Story found success in politics, however. He was elected to the Massachusetts legislature several times and was appointed to fill a vacancy in the U.S. Congress in 1808. In 1810 Story argued a case before the U.S. Supreme Court. One year later, President James Madison appointed him to the U.S. Supreme Court, making him the youngest justice ever to serve on the Court. In 1829 Story became a professor of law at Harvard, a position he held while still serving on the Supreme Court. He wrote several books about law, including his three-volume *Commentaries on the Constitution of the United States*. He served on the Court and as professor of law until his death in 1845.

In this excerpt from his *Commentaries*, Story examines the origins of the First Amendment and argues that the guarantees of free speech and a free press are not absolute.

A bill of rights is an important protection against unjust and oppressive conduct on the part of the people themselves.

Joseph Story, *Commentaries on the Constitution of the United States*. Boston: Charles C. Little and James Brown, 1851.

In a government modified, like that of the United States, (said a great statesman), the great danger lies rather in the abuse of the community, than of the legislative body. The prescriptions in favor of liberty ought to be levelled against that quarter where the greatest danger lies, namely,—that which possesses the highest prerogative of power. But this is not found in the executive or legislative departments of government; but in the body of the people, operating by the majority against the minority. It may be thought, that all paper barriers against the power of the community are too weak to be worthy of attention. They are not so strong, as to satisfy all, who have seen and examined thoroughly the texture of such a defence. Yet, as they have a tendency to impress some degree of respect for them, to establish the public opinion in their favor, and to rouse the attention of the whole community, it may be one means to control the majority from those acts, to which they might be otherwise inclined. . . .

Let us now enter upon the consideration of the amendments, which, it will be found, principally regard subjects properly belonging to a bill of rights.

The first is, "Congress shall make no law respecting an establishment of religion, or prohibiting the free exercise thereof; or abridging the freedom of speech, or of the press; or the right of the people peaceably to assemble, and to petition government for a redress of grievances.". . .

LIBERTY OF THE PRESS

That [the second clause of] this amendment was intended to secure to every citizen an absolute right to speak, or write, or print, whatever he might please, without any responsibility, public or private therefor, is a supposition too wild to be indulged by any rational man. This would be to allow to every citizen a right to destroy at his pleasure the reputation, the peace, the property, and even the personal safety of every other citizen. A man might out of mere malice and revenge, accuse another of the most infamous crimes; might excite against him the indignation of all his fellow citizens by the most atrocious calumnies; might disturb, nay, overturn all his domestic peace, and embitter his parental affections; might inflict the most distressing punishments upon the weak, the timid, and the innocent; might prejudice all a man's civil, and political, and private rights; and might stir up sedition, rebellion, and treason even against the government itself, in the wantonness of his passions, or the corruption of his heart. Civil society could not go on under such circumstances. Men would then be obliged to resort to private vengeance, to make up for the deficiencies of the law; and assassinations and savage cruelties would be perpetrated with all the frequency belonging to barbarous and brutal communities. It is plain, then, that the language of this amendment imports no more than that every man shall have

Liberty of the Press

George Hay was a Virginia legislator who served as a U.S. attorney under Thomas Jefferson and later served as a federal judge.

In this excerpt from Two Essays on the Liberty of the Press, *Hay argues that the wording of the First Amendment precludes Congress from regulating speech or the press in any way.*

To ascertain what the "freedom of the press" is, we have only to ascertain what freedom itself is. For, surely, it will be conceded, that freedom applied to one subject, means the same, as freedom applied to another subject.

Now freedom is of two kinds, and of two kinds only: one is, that absolute freedom which belongs to man, previous to any social institution; and the other, that qualified or abridged freedom, which he is content to enjoy, for the sake of government and society. I believe there is no other sort of freedom in which man is concerned.

The absolute freedom then, or what is the same thing,

a right to speak, write, and print his opinions upon any subject whatsoever, without any prior restraint, so always, that he does not injure any other person in his rights, person, property, or reputation; and so always, that he does not thereby disturb the public peace, or attempt to subvert the government. It is neither more nor less than an expansion of the great doctrine recently brought into operation in the law of libel, that every man shall be at liberty to publish what is true, with good motives and for justifiable ends. And with this reasonable limitation it is not only right in itself, but it is an inestimable privilege in a free government. Without such a limitation, it might become the scourge of the republic, first denouncing the principles of liberty, and then by rendering the most virtuous pa-

the freedom, belonging to man before any social compact, is the power uncontrouled by law, of doing what he pleases, *provided be does no injury to any other individual.* If this definition of freedom be applied to the press, as surely it ought to be, the press, if I may personify it, may do whatever it pleases to do, uncontrouled by any law, *taking care however to do no injury to any individual.* This injury can only be by slander or defamation, and reparation should be made for it in a state of nature as well as society. . . .

This argument may be summed up in a few words. The word "freedom" has meaning. It is either absolute, that is exempt from all law, or it is qualified, that is, regulated by law. . . . If it is to be regulated by law, the amendment which declares that Congress shall make no law to abridge the freedom of the press, which freedom however may be regulated by law, is the grossest absurdity that ever was conceived by the human mind.

George Hay, *Two Essays on the Liberty of the Press.* New York: De Capo Press, 1970.

triots odious through the terrors of the press, introducing despotism in its worst form.

GOVERNMENT CONTROL OF PRINTING

A little attention to the history of other countries in other ages, will teach us the vast importance of this right. It is notorious, that even to this day, in some foreign countries, it is a crime to speak on any subject, religious, philosophical, or political, what is contrary to the received opinions of the government, or the institutions of the country, however laudable may be the design, and however virtuous may be the motive. Even to animadvert upon the conduct of public men, of rulers, or representatives, in terms of the strictest truth and courtesy, has been, and is deemed a scandal upon the supposed sanctity of their stations and characters, subjecting the party to grievous punishment. In some countries no works can be printed at all, whether of science, or literature, or philosophy, without the previous approbation of the government; and the press has been shackled, and compelled to speak only in the timid language, which the cringing courtier, or the capricious inquisitor, should license for publication. The Bible itself, the common inheritance not merely of christendom, but of the world, has been put exclusively under the control of government, and not allowed to be seen or heard, except in a language unknown to the common inhabitants of the country. To publish a translation in the vernacular tongue, has been in former times a flagrant offence.

The history of the jurisprudence of England, (the most free and enlightened of all monarchies,) on this subject, will abundantly justify this statement. The art of printing, soon after its introduction, (we are told,) was locked upon, as well in England as in other countries, as merely a matter of state, and subject to the coercion of the crown. It was therefore regulated in England by the king's proclamations, prohibitions, charters of privilege, and licenses, and finally by the decrees of the court of star chamber; which limited the number of printers, and of presses, which each should employ, and prohibited new publications, unless previously approved by proper licensers. On the demolition of this odious jurisdiction, in 1641, the long parliament of Charles the First, after their rupture with that prince, assumed the same powers which the star chamber exercised with respect to licensing books; and during the commonwealth, (such is human frailty, and the love of power, even in republics!) they issued their ordinances for that purpose, founded principally upon a star chamber decree, in 1637. After the restoration of Charles the Second, a statute on the same subject was passed, copied, with some few alterations, from the parliamentary ordinances. The act expired in 1679, and was revived and continued for a few years after the revolution of 1688. Many attempts were made by the government to keep it in force; but it was so strongly resisted by parliament, that it expired in 1694, and has never since been revived. To this very hour the liberty of the press in England stands upon this negative foundation. The power to restrain it is dormant, not dead. It has never constituted an article of any of her numerous bills of rights; and that of the revolution of 1688; after securing other civil and political privileges, left this without notice, as unworthy of care, or fit for restraint.

TOO MUCH FREEDOM?

This short review exhibits, in a striking light, the gradual progress of opinion in favor of the liberty of publishing and printing opinions in England, and the frail and uncertain tenure by which it has been held. Down to this very day it is a contempt of parliament, and a high breach of privilege, to publish the speech of any member of either house, without its consent. It is true, that it is now silently established by the course of popular opinion to be innocent in practice, though not in law. But it is notorious, that within the last fifty years the publication was connived at, rather than allowed; and that for a considerable time the reports were given in a stealthy manner, covered up under the garb of speeches in a fictitious assembly.

There is a good deal of loose reasoning on the subject of the liberty of the press, as if its inviolability were constitutionally such, that, like the king of England, it could do no wrong, and was free from every inquiry, and afforded a perfect sanctuary for every abuse; that, in short, it implied a despotic sovereignty to do every sort of wrong, without the slightest accountability to private or public justice. Such a notion is too extravagant to be held by any sound constitutional lawyer, with regard to the rights and duties belonging to governments generally, or to the state governments in particular. If it were admitted to be correct, it might be justly affirmed, that the liberty of the press was incompatible with the permanent existence of any free government. Mr. Justice Blackstone has remarked, that the liberty of the press, properly understood, is essential to the nature of a free state; but that this consists in laying no *previous* restraints upon publications, and not in freedom from censure for criminal matter, when published. . . .

De Lolme states the same view of the subject; and, indeed, the liberty of the press, as understood by all England, is the right to publish without any previous restraint, or license; so, that neither the courts of justice, nor other persons, are authorized to take notice of writings intended for the press; but are confined to those which are printed. And, in such cases, if their character is questioned, whether they are lawful, or libellous, is to be tried by a jury, according to due proceedings at law. The noblest patriots of England, and the most distinguished friends of liberty, both in parliament and at the bar, have never contended for a total exemption from responsibility, but have asked only, that the guilt or innocence of the publication should be ascertained by a trial by jury.

It would seem, that a very different view of the subject was taken by a learned American commentator, though it is not, perhaps, very easy to ascertain the exact extent of his opinions. In one part of his disquisitions, he seems broadly to contend, that the security of the freedom of the press requires, that it should be exempt, not only from previous restraint by the executive, as in Great Britain; but, from legislative restraint also; and that this exemption, to be effectual, must be an exemption, not only from the previous inspection of licensers, but from the subsequent penalty of laws. In other places, he seems as explicitly to admit, that the liberty of the press does not include the right to do injury to the reputation of another, or to take from him the enjoyment of his rights or property, or to justify slander and calumny upon him, as a private or public man. And yet it is added, that every individual certainly has a right to speak, or publish his sentiments on the measures of government. To do this without restraint, control, or *fear of punishment for so doing*, is that which constitutes the genuine freedom of the press. . . .

BOUNDARIES OF FREE SPEECH

Is it contended that the liberty of the press is so much more valuable than all other rights in society, that the public safety, nay, the existence of the government itself, is to yield to it? Is private redress for libels and calumny more important, or more valuable, than the maintenance of the good order, peace, and safety, of society? It would be difficult to answer these questions in favor of the liberty of the press, without at the same time declaring, that such a licentiousness belonged, and could belong only to a despotism; and was utterly incompatible with the principles of a free government.

Besides:—What is meant by restraint of the press, or an abridgment of its liberty? If to publish, without control or responsibility, be its genuine meaning; is not that equally violated by allowing a private compensation for damages, as by a public fine? Is not a man as much restrained from doing a thing by the fear of heavy damages, as by public punishment? Is he not often as severely punished by one as by the other? Surely, it can make no difference in the case, what is the nature or extent of the restraint, if all restraint is prohibited? The legislative power is just as much prohibited from one mode as from another. And, it may be asked, where is the ground for distinguishing between public and private amenability for the wrong? The prohibition itself states no distinction. It is general; it is universal. Why, then, is the distinction attempted to be made? Plainly, because of the monstrous consequences flowing from such a doctrine. It would prostrate all personal liberty, all private peace, all enjoyment of property and good reputation. These are the great objects for which government is instituted; and, if the licentiousness of the press must endanger, not only these, but all public rights and public liberties, is it not as plain, that the right of government to punish the violators of them (the only mode of redress which it can pursue) flows from the primary duty of self-preservation? No one can doubt the importance, in a free government of a right to canvass the acts of public men, and the tendency of public measures, to censure boldly the conduct of rulers, and to scrutinize closely the policy and plans of the government. This is the great security of a free government. If we would preserve it, public opinion must be enlightened; political vigilance must be inculcated; free, but not licentious discussion, must be encouraged. But the exercise of a right is essentially different from an abuse of it. The one is no legitimate inference from the other. Common sense here promulgates the broad doctrine . . . [to] exercise your own freedom as not to infringe the rights of others, or the public peace and safety.

The Original Intent of the First Amendment

STANLEY C. BRUBAKER

In a 1980s conference paper on the Bill of Rights, Stanley C. Brubaker, a professor of political science at Colgate University, analyzes the historical context of the Bill of Rights in order to better understand the original intent of the First Amendment. Brubaker contends that the Bill of Rights was created mainly as a concession to politicians who were unwilling to ratify the Constitution without some guarantees that federal power would be limited. He sees the modern attempt to cast the First Amendment as a guiding principle for democracy that takes precedence over other competing interests as a romantic concept without a basis in history. In fact, since the Bill of Rights contains no clear definition of free speech, Brubaker argues that attempts to identify the intentions of the framers of the Constitution are mostly a matter of conjecture. Brubaker adds that the framers could not have foreseen many modern social developments that have come to shape the contemporary meaning of the First Amendment.

W hat do we mean by original intent? What was that original intent regarding the free speech and press clauses? To what extent, if any, is this intent or some other intent authoritative? I understand my primary task to concern the second question, though to make this inquiry intelligible I must adopt a preliminary answer to the question of what "original intent" means, and to make it significant, I must ad-

Stanley C. Brubaker, "Original Intent and Freedom of Speech and Press," *The Bill of Rights: Original Meaning and Current Understanding*, edited by Eugene W. Hickok Jr. Charlottesville: University Press of Virginia, 1991. Copyright © 1991 by the Rector and Visitors of the University of Virginia. Reproduced by permission.

dress the question of what authority original intent has.

The meaning of "original intent," quite apart from what role it should play in constitutional interpretation, has become a closely analyzed and warmly disputed area of constitutional theory, so I think it is necessary at the outset to make explicit, without becoming overly technical, what I mean when I use the term. For a preliminary definition, I will use the term in a way which I think will do violence neither to the sense urged by advocates of a jurisprudence of original intention nor to the conventions of contemporary language philosophers. That is, I will define it as the meaning of the clauses in question as understood by the adopters. By "adopters" I mean all who cast a vote which would determine whether or not the words should become part of the Constitution. By "meaning"—this, of course, is the trickier part—I mean what the linguists call "utterance meaning," that is, the combination of semantics (meaning of the words) and pragmatics (the context in which the words were used). And finally, by "semantics," I again will follow contemporary linguists and say that we understand the meaning of words through other words. Thus, we are looking for the sort of criteria that the adopters had in mind in 1789 when they spoke of a freedom of speech and the press, that is, the conditions *a, b*, and *c* that would need to be met if they were to call a press free. There remains the problem that only individuals, not groups, have concrete semantic intentions in an "utterance meaning," but we shall look for the core criteria that allowed the legislators to believe that they understood each other when they spoke of free speech and press.

Unfortunately for devotees of exacting notions of original intent, but fortunately for ease of summation, we do not have access to the minds of each of the adopters. I will consider, as a proxy, what was said by those who were spokesmen in the debate and the sources upon which these spokesmen seem to have relied. To simplify things further, I will not distinguish between speech and press (except when necessary), and I will focus on what is usually agreed to be of central importance, the original intent regarding political speech, especially concerning the doctrine of seditious libel: the crime of defaming the government, its officers, or its policies.

A ROMANTIC UNDERSTANDING OF THE FIRST AMENDMENT

There exists what we might call a romantic understanding of the original intent of the First Amendment's speech and press clauses. We usually hear a version of this from our students when we ask them what the First Amendment means. We are told that the First Amendment was given pride of place in the Bill of Rights in order to emphasize the bedrock importance of free speech in the country; and this bedrock importance, we discover, amounts to the principle that one should be free to do whatever he wants to do just so long as he doesn't hurt anybody—with "hurt" meaning a palpable harm, not just an offense—and as a corollary that no one should be allowed to impose his values on another, and, certainly, the government shouldn't be allowed to impose its values on anybody. And if we ask if liberty of speech is distinct from license of speech, we are likely to be told that the clause was intended to abolish such distinctions. From scholars and justices of the twentieth century, we have heard a more sophisticated version of this same understanding. [In a 1941 book] Professor [Zechariah] Chafee told us that the framers' intent was "to wipe out the common law of sedition, and make further prosecutions for criticism of the government, without any incitement of law-breaking, forever impossible in the United States of America"; that with the Sedition Act of 1798, small-minded men choked the expansive protection of free speech with wicked doctrines; that [Supreme Court justice Oliver Wendell] Holmes breathed new life into the document, reviving its original spirit with his eloquent dissents, the general thrust of which constitutes today's law. Perhaps the most exemplary of these dissents is that of *Gitlow v. New York* [1925], where he wrote: "If in the long run the beliefs expressed in proletarian dictatorship are destined to be accepted by the dominant forces of the community, the only meaning of free speech is that they should be given their chance and have their way."

We probably will continue to hear versions of original intent such as these from beginning students, and we will no doubt continue to hear such ideas put forward by scholars and justices as the central meaning of free speech. But since 1960, none has been able to claim plausibly that if this is the only meaning of free speech, it is the one intended by those who wrote and ratified the First Amendment. That year was when Leonard Levy published *Legacy of Suppression*. Drawing largely upon this work by Levy, as he has revised it in his 1985 edition, we have a reasonably clear idea of what the adopters must have had in mind when they used the term "freedom of speech and press."

To begin, we should consider the pragmatics, or the context of the free speech and press clause. For the framers there was no intention of emphasizing a firstness of the speech and press clauses by placing them in the First Amendment. In [James] Madison's original submission of a bill of rights, free press protections were listed twice—one protecting the press against state government, the other against national government—but in neither case was speech protection first. In fact, Madison did not really intend for these amendments to be listed as a distinct bill of rights but rather to be interspersed in appropriate places in the Constitution. These amendments, seventeen in number, as slightly revised by the special House committee and on the House floor, were sent to the Senate. There the restriction on state infringement of freedom of the press was dropped and the restriction on the federal government, apparently for stylistic reasons only, was combined with those protecting religious liberty, forming what was returned to the House as the Third Amendment, in which position it remained when submitted to the states, emerging as our First Amendment only when the original first two failed to secure the support of three-quarters of the states. Perhaps it should come as no great surprise that a free press clause was not first when we consider that of the twelve states ratifying the Constitution before the Bill of Rights was considered, only three recommended such a provision.

As for the primary intention behind these clauses, and the Bill of Rights generally, it seems that ratifying a bill of rights was merely incidental to other political intentions. Anti-Federalists pointed to the absence of a bill of rights in order to drum up further opposition to the Constitution that they would have rejected in any case. The Federalists responded that a bill of rights was unnecessary as the Constitution authorized only the enumerated powers and thus the federal government had no authority to abridge such rights in the first place. Only when it seemed that the Constitution would fail if pledges were not made to adopt a bill of rights did leading Federalists make such pledges. But here, too, the motivation was less the bill of rights than how it would affect the strength of the new government. Madison and others believed, no doubt correctly, that if Congress did not approve a bill of rights, the Federalists might not be able to halt the move for a new constitutional convention which would significantly curtail the authority of the new Constitution. Since a new convention was exactly what the Anti-Federalists wanted, they voiced no great enthusiasm for this bill of rights, the want of which they had so shrilly decried during the ratification debates. In the midst of this struggle, against the unremitting apathy of the Federalists and the baffled opposition of the Anti-Federalists, Madison confided to a colleague his principal motivation in urging the amendments. Though he thought there was nothing "improper" in the amendments, and perhaps they might produce some good, he found the project of gaining support for the amendments was "nauseous." But the amendments "will kill the opposition everywhere, and by putting an end to disaffection to the Government itself, enable the administration to venture on measures not otherwise safe." As Levy writes: "Our precious Bill of Rights, at least in its immediate background, resulted from the reluctant necessity of certain Federalists to capitalize on a cause that had been originated, in vain, by the Anti-Federalists for ulterior party purposes. The party that had first opposed the Bill of Rights inadvertently wound up with the responsibility for its framing and ratification, while the party that had first professedly wanted it discovered too late that it not only was embarrassing but disastrous for those ulterior purposes."

In so describing the motivations of the Federalists and Anti-Federalists, I do not mean to denigrate their concern for the liberties that we find in the Bill of Rights. Rather, I mean to emphasize that both saw the form of government, more than any parchment barrier appended to it, as the guarantor of rights. As [Alexander] Hamilton said in *The Federalist* No. 84, the Constitution itself is a bill of rights. And for the Anti-Federalists, following classical republicanism, only in a small republic could liberties remain secure. Still, beyond their pragmatic intention, the framers and adopters had a semantic intention, and it is to this we now turn.

WHAT IS MEANT BY FREE SPEECH?

The debates in Congress concerning the speech and press clauses shed scant light on the question of meaning. The Senate kept no records of its debates, so that we can only make sketchy inferences from motions accepted and rejected. We do know, for instance, that the Senate rejected a motion to specify the protection of free speech as "ample . . . as hath at any time been secured by the common law." But we cannot infer much from this. The Senate might have thought it too narrow or too confusing a definition of free speech, or it might simply have regarded the phrase as unnecessary. And for reasons that remain a mystery, the Senate changed the House restriction on the federal government generally to a restriction on Congress alone: "Congress shall make no law. . . ." On the House floor, where Madison introduced his bill of rights, there was only a brief exchange concerning free speech. This occurred when the Federalists fought back a move to insert into the right of assembly the doctrine of instructions. Madison simply affirmed that the free speech clause would encompass the right of the people "to express and communicate their sentiments and wishes" to their representatives.

Nor do we find enlightening comments in the state legislatures that considered the amendments or the local newspapers or pamphlets of the time. To be sure, there was lavish praise for freedom of speech, but, according to Levy, "no one seems to have cared enough to clarify what he meant by the subject upon which he lavished praise." But in a way this very lack of debate on the scope of meaning of free speech is helpful, for it suggests that there was a commonly shared understanding of what was meant, and if so, that understanding is almost certainly the one existing in the common law as it had been applied in the states. If the free speech clause had deviated from what was the established law, surely there would have been some debate about it. This common-law understanding is given in a well-known passage from [eighteenth-century English jurist Sir William] Blackstone (echoes of which resounded throughout America in the colonial. Revolutionary, and founding eras):

> The liberty of the press is indeed essential to the nature of a free state; but this consists in laying no *previous* restraints upon publications, and not in freedom from censure for criminal matter when published. Every freeman has an undoubted right to lay what sentiments he pleases before the public; to forbid this is to destroy the freedom of the press: but if he publishes what is improper, mischievous, or illegal, he must take the consequences of his own temerity. . . . To punish (as the law does at present) any dangerous or offensive writings, which, when published, shall on a fair and impartial trial be adjudged of a pernicious tendency, is necessary for the preservation of peace and good order, a government and religion, the only solid foundations of civil liberty. Thus the will of the individuals is still left free; the abuse only of that free-will is the object of legal punishment. Neither is any restraint hereby laid upon freedom of thought or enquiry: liberty of private sentiments is still left; the disseminating, or making public, of bad sentiments, destructive of the ends of society, is the crime which society corrects.

And this scope of free press does not differ in any significant way from that advocated by the major theorists who might have influenced the framers—Locke, Spinoza, Trenchard and Gordon, Milton.

BEYOND THE COMMON LAW INTERPRETATION

There exist some indications that the adopters intended to go beyond the Blackstonian statement of the common law. Four are worthy of consideration. First, the [eighteenth-century journalist and painter John Peter] Zenger trial of 1735 had gained some support for the notion that truth should serve as a defense against a libel charge and that juries rather than the judges should determine whether the words in question were libelous.[1] And, loosely tied to these developments, there was some support for the proposition that, contrary to the common-law tradition, good motives could exculpate one from a charge of libel. Yet, as Levy notes, during the era of the American Revolution, "no state, despite its new freedom, adopted the Zengerian reforms," and at the time of the founding "Zengerian principles had few open advocates."

Second is the possibility of literalism, suggesting that the words "no law" meant that the federal government should have nothing to do with the freedom of the press. That it would not, except for copyright, was, of course, the response of the Federalists to the contention of the Anti-Federalists that the Constitution was defective in lacking a bill of rights. Pursuing the logic of this position, the Federalists argued that it would be dangerous to have such a limit where there was never intended to be any authority. A bill of rights, wrote Hamilton in *The Federalist* No. 84, "would contain various exceptions to powers which are not granted; and, on this very account, would afford a colorable pretext to claim more than were granted. For why declare that things not be done which there is not power to do? Why, for instance, should it be said that the liberty of the press shall not be restrained when no power is given by which

---

1. Ignoring the instructions of the judge, a jury acquitted printer John Peter Zenger of libel charges on the grounds that what he had printed was true and factual.

restrictions may be imposed?" At least with hindsight, the Federalist claim appears patently defective, for clearly in the name of several of the enumerated powers—commerce, tax, raising an army—it is possible to abridge freedom of the press. And further, it is no doubt necessary for the federal government to restrict speech. As [former solicitor general and U.S. Court of Appeals judge] Robert Bork asks rhetorically, "Is Congress forbidden to prohibit incitement to mutiny aboard a naval vessel engaged in action against an enemy, to prohibit shouted harangues from the visitors gallery during its own deliberations or to provide any rules for decorum in the federal courtrooms?" But that the federal government would have no power over speech and the press was a stated position and a repeated one, and perhaps it was believed by some.

Still, even if the no power at all interpretation of the clause is true, it does little to forward an expansive free speech doctrine. For no one doubted that the press needed to be restrained, and thus such a reading would carry the corollaries (a) that the business of press restriction is emphatically the business of the state, and if so, then (b) incorporating the First Amendment into the Fourteenth becomes a logical impossibility. I doubt, however, that this is an accurate understanding of the intentions of the adopters, for the more the proposed constitution was considered, the less plausible the Federalist argument seemed. Further, many of the states had wording similar to that of the First Amendment, and they were not understood to have the absolute meanings suggested here.

Pursuing the claim of literalism, what about the opening words, "Congress shall make no law . . ."? Did the adopters intend this literally? Possibly, but the observation seems most likely to count for a common-law scope of freedom of the press. As mentioned above, there was a move in the Senate to define the freedom of the press as identical to that of the common law. That failed. But perhaps its proponents did not stop there and carried their efforts into the committee where the broad language of the House, affirming the freedom of the press against all aspects of the federal government, was narrowed at "Congress." James Wilson [a member of the first U.S. Supreme Court] thought that the Constitution affirmed a common-law cognizance of criminal cases in the federal courts, and so did every member of the Supreme Court before whom the question was raised before 1812, save Samuel Chase in 1798, who within a year changed his position to affirm that of his fellow justices, and these cases included a case of seditious libel. That also is the conclusion of [constitutional scholar] Charles Warren's exemplary study of the Judiciary Act of 1798. Whether this was intended to be a federal common law or state common law is, of course, a matter of continuing controversy, but on the question of the protection afforded freedom of speech the controversy has little bearing, for on this point the common law was virtually the same in all the states.

The third possibility for an understanding broader than that at common law focuses on press practices of the time. These were indeed more expansive than press law and press theories of the time, and this observation forms the basis for Levy's somewhat more liberal conclusions in his revised study. "When the framers of the First Amendment provided that Congress shall not abridge the freedom of the press they could only have meant to protect the press with which they were familiar and as it operated at the time. They constitutionally guaranteed the practice of freedom of the press." But as he admits in his preface, practice does not dictate the meaning of the concept. "In our own time, obscenity is still illegal, though we live in a society saturated by it and witness few prosecutions; their paucity does not illumine the meaning of obscenity. So, too, the rarity of prosecutions for seditious libel, and the existence of an unfettered press do not illumine the scope and meaning of freedom of the press or the law on freedom of the press."

Finally, in favor of a more expansive interpretation, commentators turn to the resistance to the Sedition Act,[2] which involved several men we count as framers, including James Madi-

2. One of four laws passed by Congress in 1798 in response to hostile actions by the French revolutionary government. The Sedition Act prohibited many kinds of criticism of the government, Congress, or the president.

son. And here we do find arguments for a more liberal interpretation of the First Amendment's free speech and press clauses than that which existed at the common law. But two points need to be made. First, as Walter Berns has convincingly demonstrated—and Levy has not effectively refuted him—the primary concern of the opponents of the Sedition Act was not freedom of the press but freedom of the states, which included a freedom to regulate the press and punish libel as they saw appropriate. And second, in looking to the comments we have shifted our focus from original intent to the evolving intent of the originators. Comments made in the heat of the controversy of 1798–1800 provided little insight about the thinking of 1789.

On the intentions of the adopters, we can say in summation, that while there are areas of ambiguity, if we are looking for the criteria meaning that the adopters had in their minds, one cannot possibly claim that it followed the romantic vision mentioned above, and one cannot possibly disclaim that it simply embraced the common-law understanding of free press.

A Gulf Between Original Intent and Modern Interpretation

A rather striking conclusion is thus forced on us. Between the most generous interpretation of this original intent and the most restrictive view that we find expressed by justices and scholars today, there lies a gulf. What then lies between us and them that leads to such incompatible conclusions when we look to the same words? Do we know something that they did not know? Did they know something that we've forgotten? To the latter two questions, I think that the answer is yes and yes. We do know something that they didn't. For one thing, the distinction between opposition to a regime and opposition to policies or leaders within a regime as the basis for a political party is so clear to us today that [George] Washington's Farewell Address warning us "in the most solemn manner against the baneful effects of the spirit of party" seems almost quaint. Animadversion directed toward throwing the rascals out is now easier to distinguish from animadversion directed toward overthrowing the regime, and far easier to tolerate. And when this distinction is coupled with the realization that the regime is in a sense the people themselves, the place for a doctrine of seditious libel becomes more narrowly defined. Of course, the framers knew these things in the abstract, but they had to be proved as historical facts—and more significantly as historical possibilities—before they could supply a knowledgeable foundation for the expansion of free speech. Upon them can comfortably rest our familiar arguments: that speech must be expansively protected if we are to have informed voting, if public affairs will be genuine affairs of the public, if public officials can be held responsible for their actions, if abuses of power are to be discovered. Only upon the knowledge that a people can govern itself can one sensibly argue that freedom of speech is the very matrix of all our other liberties.

But the adopters also knew some things that we seem to have forgotten. For one thing, they understood the sense in which freedom of speech is meaningless unless tied to self-government, using that term in both its public and personal sense. That is, they understood that a coherent sense of self, an identity, must logically precede freedom, for an act is free only if it is self-generated. In short, freedom presupposes character, and character presupposes self-discipline or self-government. But self-discipline is not self-acquired. It is virtually impossible without cultivation by family, society, and, at least indirectly, government.

Similarly, the action of the government is free only if it proceeds from a coherent identity of the public self. It was this very lack of coherence that had moved Madison and the other key actors to form the Constitution; repeatedly one finds in the writings of the leading framers concern with the inconstancy of the state governments, the mutability of their laws. Thus the primary concern of the framers with the form of government—structuring, as is necessary with individual identity, its elements in a proper, stable, and coherent fashion—and their relative inattention to parchment statements of rights. And the framers were probably correct in their judgment that a press which inflamed the passions, exciting fear, jealousy, or hatred of the government and its leaders, could not help the cause of deliberative identity and thus could not aid the cause of free government.

Self-government for the framers entailed the distinction—repeated in virtually all pre-twentieth-century discussions of freedom of speech—between liberty and license. Without that distinction, the cultivation of individual identity and the structuring of the elements of political power are both utterly arbitrary; all restraints on the individual become tyrannical, and obedience to the laws becomes servility. In sum, they realized that liberty is worthless unless there is some good and truth to be pursued.

One major lesson we should learn from the framers, then, is that many common expressions of support for an expansive interpretation of freedom of speech and press invoke not a philosophy of self-government but one of nihilistic relativism. Consider Holmes's famous obiter dictum in *Gitlow* quoted above: "If in the long run the beliefs expressed in proletarian dictatorship are destined to be accepted by the dominant forces of the community, the only meaning of free speech is that they should be given their chance and have their way." Free speech stands on the same status as dictatorship of the proletariat; whatever time brings is right. Or consider the philosophical reflections that open Levy's exhaustive work: "Neither freedom of speech nor of press could become a civil liberty until people believed that the truth of their opinions, especially their religious opinions was relative rather than absolute." If all opinions are relative, then the opinion in favor of freedom of speech is itself relative. At this point, where liberty is indistinguishable from license, it suddenly transforms to nihilism, for if all opinions are relative, then nothing is forbidden and all is permitted.

DOES ORIGINAL INTENT STILL HAVE AUTHORITY?

This reflection suggests another question. If we are not bound by original intent, are we unbound? Is everything, as a matter of constitutional interpretation, permitted? Can we add to the things that the adopters knew the things that they didn't know, without abandoning all ground of authority? Again, we must return to the questions that I dealt with perfunctorily at the outset: What do we mean by "original intent"? and, Is there a conception of it that is authoritative?

A theory of the Constitution which takes seriously a theory of original intent must give careful attention to the adopters' interpretive intent: How did they intend the document to be interpreted? In this regard, we should note the approach that Madison took in regard to the free press clause. A decade after the adoption of the First Amendment, Madison advocated a meaning of free press which it is hard to imagine was in the minds of most Americans, including his own, in 1789. As part of the Jeffersonian response to the Sedition Act of 1798, Madison repudiated a significant component of the common-law understanding of seditious libel, libel of the government itself. Arguing from the form of government, he maintained that the Blackstonian understanding of free speech, appropriate for a country based on sovereignty of the legislature, is not appropriate for a country based on sovereignty of the people. Where in Britain the sovereign Parliament maintains rights against the prerogative of the king, in America, the sovereign people must maintain their rights against the government. Intelligent selection of representatives and informed judgment of their conduct are utterly dependent on a free press, Madison maintained, and "the right of electing the members of the Government constitutes . . . the essence of free and responsible government." That is to say, Madison did not base his interpretation of free speech, either at the federal or state level, on the specific intentions of the adopters but on his best understanding of the true meaning of free speech in a democratic republic.

We should note as well that the authority sought and won by *The Federalist Papers* rests upon a similar sort of claim. The authority and respect accorded to Publius's[3] explication of the

3. Publius is the pseudonym used by Alexander Hamilton, James Madison, and John Jay, the authors of *The Federalist Papers.*

Constitution derives not from his intimate knowledge of specific intentions—which was never claimed—but from his patriotism, comprehension of America's historical situation, and, most important, his profound understanding of the nature of republican government. If the identity of Publius had never been revealed, I think we would be foolish to regard his arguments as any less persuasive or authoritative than we do today.

It follows from this observation that my preliminary definition of "original intent" is defective, at least upon its own terms. This definition accepted the "criteria" understanding of meaning, following the apparent sense of some advocates of original jurisprudence and contemporary language philosophy. For most of the latter, how we divide up the world and the names we attach to those divisions are merely matters of convention. For the framers, the adopters, and I think for a coherent theory of the Constitution, on the other hand, there is a nature to the divisions, a nature to republican government, and a nature to freedom of speech. Original intent, properly understood, should entail out an intention to render the contemporaneous definitions of the words authoritative, but to indicate the "thing" whose nature, in light of our collective experience, we as interpreters must try to comprehend. In place of a "criteria" meaning of original intent, this approach would focus on "natural" meaning.

No doubt, it will be objected that such an understanding of original intent undermines one strong rationale for this form of jurisprudence, that is, to confine the discretion of the interpreter. And without further elaboration of the concept, the charge is certainly understandable, for it might seem to open the door to interpretations wildly divergent from what the framers intended by any reasonable understanding of "intent." Here, I can only point to *The Federalist Papers* and aspects of [Alexis de] Tocqueville's *Democracy in America* as examples of the sort of "natural" interpretation I have in mind.

Finally, I should make clear that as I understand original intent here in this revised form, the task of discovering the true meaning of the things indicated by the words of the Constitution is a task not intended for the judges alone. Indeed. on questions concerning the constitutionality of statutory law, their judgment is a secondary one, the primary one being vested with the legislators. And to avoid duplicating the legislative function, courts should follow the rule articulated by [attorney, author, and professor of law] James Bradley Thayer, to declare an act of the legislature unconstitutional only if it involves a clear mistake of constitutional meaning. If my conclusion in favor of "natural" interpretation alarms conservatives, my conclusion in favor of judicial restraint is certain to do no less for the liberals. But in both cases I think the concern is unfounded. For the reluctance of the Federalists to enact a bill of rights was not entirely unwarranted, and it remains true that the form of government is itself our strongest bill of rights.

The Supreme Court and the States Apply the First Amendment

FREDE CASTBERG

A professor and rector at the University of Oslo, Frede Castberg analyzes the historical application of the First Amendment by the U.S.
Supreme Court. In this excerpt from his 1960 book, *Freedom of
Speech in the West*, Castberg examines several of the Court's decisions
that effectively erased restrictions on speech and the press that were
tantamount to censorship. In *Near v. Minnesota*, for example, the
Court set a new standard for restraining libelous publications; in
Grosjean v. American Press Co., the Court determined that taxes could
not be used to burden or gag periodicals. Castberg also analyzes early
Supreme Court decisions regarding public assembly and canvassing.
Finally, Castberg looks at the role the Fourteenth Amendment has
played in extending the protection of free speech to the states.

The First Amendment forbids Congress to create a state
church or to hinder freedom of religion. Further, Congress
is forbidden to make laws "abridging the freedom of speech, or
of the press; or the right of the people peaceably to assemble,
and to petition the Government for a redress of grievances".

Historically, the Constitution's provisions concerning freedom of expression and printing are directed chiefly against the
censorship of printed matter prior to its publication. Many authors of the age of enlightenment considered "liberty of the
press" to be synonymous with a ban on such censorship.

Frede Castberg, *Freedom of Speech in the West: A Comparative Study of Public Law in France,
the United States, and Germany.* Oslo, Norway: Oslo University Press, 1960. Copyright
© 1960 by Oslo University Press. All rights reserved. Reproduced by permission.

CENSORSHIP

The Supreme Court has on several occasions rigidly maintained that prohibition of "previous restraints" which in this respect was the chief purpose of the First Amendment. An interesting and significant decision was reached in the case of *Near v. Minnesota* in 1931. The case concerned the publishers of a newspaper which was violently anti-Semitic, endorsed the Ku Klux Klan, and made very strong charges against the law enforcement officers of the state. Chief Justice [Charles Evans] Hughes, who delivered the opinion of the Court, pointed out that the statute concerned in fact put the publisher under an effective censorship. The statute established that a newspaper or periodical which was found to be "malicious, scandalous, and defamatory" could be suppressed; resumption of publication then was punishable as a contempt of court. The operation and effect of the statute was, in the opinion of the Chief Justice, that public authorities may bring the owner or publisher of a newspaper or periodical before a judge upon a charge of conducting a business of publishing scandalous and defamatory matter—in particular that the matter consists of charges against public officers of official dereliction. Unless the owner or publisher was able and disposed to bring competent evidence to satisfy the judge that the charges were true and were published with good motives and for justifiable ends, his newspaper or periodical was suppressed and further publication was made punishable as a contempt. This is of the essence of censorship.

The Supreme Court has also struck at other forms of "previous restraint" of periodical publications. The case of *Grosjean v. American Press Co.* of 1936 concerned amongst other things the question of whether the Constitution's provision on the liberty of the press is a protection against a licence tax for the privilege of engaging in the business of "selling, or making any charge for, advertising". Justice [George] Sutherland, speaking first, gave a detailed account of how in England in the 18th century the imposition of taxes had been used as a means of gagging the press. The provisions in the First Amendment aimed also at such "modes of restraint" as the one here considered. The tax here involved was bad, "because, in the light of its history and of its present setting, it is seen to be a deliberate and calculated device in the guise of a tax to limit the circulation of information to which the public is entitled in virtue of the constitutional guaranties". The Justice also declared that "the form in which the tax is imposed is in itself suspicious . . . It is measured alone by the extent of the circulation of the publication in which the advertisements are carried, with the plain purpose of penalizing the publishers and curtailing the circulation of a selected group of newspapers". . . .

PUBLIC ASSEMBLY

Street demonstrations and the distribution of agitatory documents in public places are also considered to be protected by the provision of the First Amendment. An official system of control with compulsory licensing is now deemed by the Supreme Court to be censorship contrary to the Constitution.

This has not always been the point of view of the Supreme Court. A judgment of 1897, in *Davis v. Massachusetts*, maintained as constitutionally defensible a Boston ordinance which required a permit from the mayor for any person to "make any public address, discharge any cannon or firearm, expose for sale any goods, . . ." on public grounds: In *Hague v. Committee for Industrial Organization* the Supreme Court adopted a different standpoint. The case hinged on a city ordinance decreeing that a permit for meeting on public ground should be refused only "for the purpose of preventing riots, disturbances, or disorderly assemblage". In fact the licensing official had, in the opinion of the Supreme Court, used his authority as an "instrument of arbitrary suppression of free expression of views on national affairs".

The *Schneider v. State (Town of Irvington)* case concerned a municipal ordinance prohibiting solicitation and distribution of circulars, by canvassing from house to house, unless licensed by the police after an inquiry and decision. The Supreme Court regarded this disposition as amounting to censorship and therefore unconstitutional. The streets are natural and proper places for the dissemination of information and opinion; and one is not to have the exercise of one's liberty of expression in appropriate places abridged on the plea that it may be exercised in some other place. Here it was religious writings that were in question, but the result would have been no different, had they had political contents.

Permission in advance can be demanded, as long as it is only a question of "time, place and manner, so as to conserve the public convenience" (*Cox v. New Hampshire*). On the other hand an arrangement making propaganda activity dependent on the Mayor's finding it "proper and advisable" is an indefensible administrative censorship (*Largent v. Texas*). A typical judgment is that pronounced in *Kunz v. New York*, regarding a man who had held a religious meeting in the streets without the prescribed police permit. His earlier police permit had been withdrawn because he had ridiculed and denounced other religious opinions. It would, according to the Supreme Court, be against the constitutional provision in the First Amendment to recognize an administrative official's "restraining control over the right to speak on religious subjects" without some "appropriate standards to guide his action."

This case, too, concerned religious agitation, but political agitation is certainly protected against previous censorship to the same extent as religious agitation. . . .

APPLYING THE FIRST AMENDMENT TO THE STATES

It is via [the due process clause of the Fourteenth Amendment] that the provision in the First Amendment has been made applicable also to the individual states. That this has been able to happen is because of the fact that the due process rule has been considered to extend to certain fundamental principles of freedom, especially the provision of the First Amendment. . . .

In 1833 the Supreme Court pronounced a judgment in the case of *Barron v. Baltimore*, which explicitly repudiated the claim that the first amendments should without more ado be deemed binding for the states. The wording, in particular of the First Amendment which is addressed to Congress, argues against the idea that the intention can have been to tamper with the authority of the states.

In 1866 Congress ratified the Fourteenth Amendment, which in Section 1 forbids the states both to "make or enforce any law which shall abridge the privileges or immunities of citizens of the United States" and to "deprive any person of life, liberty, or property, without due process of law."

The Supreme Court, however, to begin with held the view that the Fourteenth Amendment by no means made the rules in the first eight amendments automatically applicable to the states. A Supreme Court judgment from 1884 in the case of *Hurtado v. California* concerned the question of whether a state was bound by the rule about a "Grand Jury" in the Fifth Amendment. The Court said no, especially bearing in mind the consideration that the words "due process of law" were co-ordinated with the Grand Jury rule in the Fifth Amendment. The same words could not then have a different meaning in the Fourteenth Amendment, so as there to embrace the Grand Jury rule.

When the question arose of the states' relation to the First Amendment on free speech, the result was, however, different. In a celebrated judgment pronounced by the Supreme Court in 1925 concerning political freedom of speech, no-one based a dissent on the ground that the First Amendment was not valid for the states. The case of *Gitlow. v. New York* concerned one of inciting to rebellion, and the conviction was sustained, against the dissent of Justices [Oliver Wendell] Holmes and [Louis] Brandeis. Yet Justice [Edward] Sanford, delivering the opinion of the Court, declared: "For the present purposes we may and do assume that freedom of speech and of the press—which are protected by the First Amendment from abridgment by Congress—are among the fundamental personal rights and "liberties" protected by the due process clause of the Fourteenth Amendment from impairment by the States. . . ."

SETTING LIMITS ON FREE SPEECH

In applying the First Amendment to the states, a decision must be reached on the question of how to set the limits to freedom of speech. Obviously there is a limit, not only for statements about private individuals, but also for statements directed against the national order. The circumstance that the First Amendment does not itself suggest anything about limits to the freedom of speech, can not reasonably mean that the legislation of the Union or of the states can never make a criminal offence of any statement about the nation or society, even if the statement is intended to provoke violence against the existing order of society. Somewhere between permissible or even sharp criticism of the government, and incitement to rebellion, a limit must be set.

Given the constitutional position of the courts in the United States, it is clear that it must be the courts, and in the final instance, the federal Supreme Court, who set this limit. And the boundary between constitutional and unconstitutional use of the freedom of speech or between permissible and not permissible legislation in this field, must necessarily include a weighing against each other of the interests and considerations which come into conflict.

The courts, and principally the Supreme Court, whose standpoint guides the other courts, are in this way again faced with problems of evaluation in which each judge must weigh incommensurable values one against the other, chiefly freedom of the spirit against the external and internal security and order of the society. The Supreme Court has not shirked such an evaluation.

There is within the court a strong tendency to apply particularly severe standards to legislation, especially state legislation, when it deals with freedom of speech—political as well as religious. While the judicial assessment of social and economic legislation has practically ceased, it is still exercised with full power for the protection of freedom of speech. In the first field the Supreme Court clearly practises "judicial restraint" and a policy of *"laissez-faire"* which benefits the legislator. In the second field, that of spiritual freedom, a so-called "judicial activism" seems to influence partly the whole court and at any rate some of its members, even finding expression occasionally in the form of a presumption that interference in spiritual freedom on the part of the legislature is at odds with the Constitution. The freedom which is based on the First Amendment belongs, according to the opinion to which Chief Justice [Harlan] Stone amongst others has given expression, to "the preferred freedoms". . . .

The First Amendment treats of clearly limited aspects of life: religious life, speech and press, assemblies and petitions. Every word used in the Article can of course raise doubts in boundary cases. But that is true of all—absolutely all—the words and concepts with which law and legal thinking operate. It is true that the limitation of the First Amendment in all the fields with which it is concerned necessitates an evaluation in the question of the boundary between the permitted and the forbidden. Naturally it would have been an advantage had the Constitution itself laid down a norm which could be decisive, or which could set a standard for deciding that question. Those constitutions, however, which are credited with the authority of great age, such as the Constitution of the United States, are frequently rather vague in their formulation of principles. And since it is, once and for all, the courts which have the authority to apply the Constitution to the work of the legislator, it must be the courts who determine where to place the limits on constitutionally guaranteed freedom.

CHAPTER 3

LANDMARK
SUPREME
COURT
DECISIONS

AMERICAN
SOCIAL
MOVEMENTS

The Doctrine of Incitement

OLIVER WENDELL HOLMES JR.

The first Supreme Court case to test the limits of the First Amendment's guarantees of free speech was *Schenck v. United States.* In the midst of World War I, Charles T. Schenck and his wife Elizabeth Baer mailed circulars to fifteen thousand young men who had been called and accepted for military service under the conscription act of May 18, 1917. The circulars urged the recipients to resist the draft. For publishing and distributing their antiwar tract, Schenck and Baer were convicted of violating the Espionage Act of June 15, 1917. They appealed, claiming that their actions were protected by the free speech clause of the First Amendment. In a unanimous decision, the Supreme Court rejected their claim, holding that a speaker who incites lawless action is not protected by the First Amendment. Justice Oliver Wendell Holmes Jr. wrote the opinion of the Court.

The son of American poet Oliver Wendell Holmes, Oliver Wendell Holmes Jr. was born in Boston in 1841. He enlisted in the Union army in 1861 and served for four years during the American Civil War. Afterwards he attended Harvard Law School, receiving a degree in 1866 and opening a practice in Boston in 1867. In 1881, Holmes earned a reputation as an important legal mind with the publication of a series of lectures he gave at the Lowell Institute. He became a professor of law at Harvard in 1882 and was appointed to the Massachusetts court a few months later. He served on the bench for twenty years. In 1902, President Theodore Roosevelt appointed Holmes to the U.S. Supreme Court. He became known as the Great Dissenter for a series of eloquent dissenting opinions he wrote urging judicial restraint. His published books include *The Common Law*

Oliver Wendell Holmes Jr., opinion, *Schenck v. United States*, 249 U.S. 47, 1919.

(1881), *Speeches* (1891, 1913), and *Collected Legal Papers* (1920). He served on the Court until 1932. Three years after retiring from the bench, he died.

This is an indictment in three counts. The first charges a conspiracy to violate the Espionage Act of June 15, 1917, . . . by causing and attempting to cause insubordination, &c., in the military and naval forces of the United States, and to obstruct the recruiting and enlistment service of the United States, when the United States was at war with the German Empire, to-wit, that the defendant wilfully conspired to have printed and circulated to men who had been called and accepted for military service under the Act of May 18, 1917, . . . a document set forth and alleged to be calculated to cause such insubordination and obstruction. The count alleges overt acts in pursuance of the conspiracy, ending in the distribution of the document set forth. The second count alleges a conspiracy to commit an offense against the United States, to-wit, to use the mails for the transmission of matter declared to be nonmailable by title 12, 2, of the Act of June 15, 1917, . . . to-wit, the above mentioned document, with an averment of the same overt acts. The third count charges an unlawful use of the mails for the transmission of the same matter and otherwise as above. The defendants were found guilty on all the counts. They set up the First Amendment to the Constitution forbidding Congress to make any law abridging the freedom of speech, or of the press, and bringing the case here on that ground have argued some other points also of which we must dispose.

THE HANDBILLS

It is argued that the evidence, if admissible, was not sufficient to prove that the defendant Schenck was concerned in sending the documents. According to the testimony Schenck said he was general secretary of the Socialist party and had charge of the Socialist headquarters from which the documents were sent. He identified a book found there as the minutes of the Executive Committee of the party. The book showed a resolution of August 13, 1917, that 15,000 leaflets should be printed on the other side of one of them in use, to be mailed to men who had passed exemption boards, and for distribution. Schenck personally attended to the printing. On August 20 the general secretary's report said 'Obtained new leaflets from printer and started work addressing envelopes' &c.; and there was a resolve that Comrade Schenck be allowed $125 for sending leaflets through the mail. He said that he had about fifteen or sixteen thousand printed. There were files of the circular in question in the inner office which he said were printed on the other side of the one sided circular and were there for distribution. Other copies were proved to have been sent through the mails to drafted men. Without going into confirmatory details that were proved, no reasonable man could doubt that the defendant Schenck was largely instrumental in sending the circulars about. As to the defendant Baer there was evidence that she was a member of the Executive Board and that the minutes of its transactions were hers. The argument as to the sufficiency of the evidence that the defendants conspired to send the documents only impairs the seriousness of the real defence.

It is objected that the documentary evidence was not admissible because obtained upon a search warrant, valid so far as appears. The contrary is established. . . . The search warrant did not issue against the defendant but against the Socialist headquarters at 1326 Arch street and it would seem that the documents technically were not even in the defendants' possession. . . . Notwithstanding some protest in argument the notion that evidence even directly proceeding from the defendant in a criminal proceeding is excluded in all cases by the Fifth Amendment is plainly unsound. . . .

THE CALL TO RESIST

The document in question upon its first printed side recited the first section of the Thirteenth Amendment, said that the idea embodied in it was violated by the conscription act and that a conscript is little better than a convict. In impassioned language it intimated that conscription was despotism in its worst form and a monstrous wrong against humanity in the interest of Wall Street's chosen few. It said, 'Do not submit to intimidation,' but in form at least confined itself to peaceful measures such as a petition for the repeal of the act. The other and later printed side of the sheet was headed 'Assert Your Rights.' It stated reasons for alleging that any one violated the Constitution when he refused to recognize 'your right to assert your opposition to the draft,' and went on, 'If you do not assert and support your rights, you are helping to deny or disparage rights which it is the solemn duty of all citizens and residents of the United States to retain.' It described the arguments on the other side as coming from cunning politicians and a mercenary capitalist press, and even silent consent to the conscription law as helping to support an infamous conspiracy. It denied the power to send our citizens away to foreign shores to shoot up the people of other lands, and added that words could not express the condemnation such cold-blooded ruthlessness deserves, &c., &c., winding up, 'You must do your share to maintain, support and uphold the rights of the people of this country.' Of course the document would not have been sent unless it had been intended to have some effect, and we do not see what effect it could be expected to have upon persons subject to the draft except to influence them to obstruct the carrying of it out. The defendants do not deny that the jury might find against them on this point.

INTENT AND CIRCUMSTANCES

But it is said, suppose that that was the tendency of this circular, it is protected by the First Amendment to the Constitution. Two of the strongest expressions are said to be quoted respectively from well-known public men. It well may be that the prohibition of laws abridging the freedom of speech is not confined to previous restraints, although to prevent them may have been the main purpose, as intimated in Patterson v. Colorado. . . . We admit that in many places and in ordinary times the defendants in saying all that was said in the circular would have been within their constitutional rights. But the character of every act depends upon the circumstances in which it is done. . . . The most stringent protection of free speech would not protect a man in falsely shouting fire in a theatre and causing a panic. It does not even protect a man from an injunction against uttering words that may have all the effect of force. . . . The question in every case is whether the words used are used in such circumstances and are of such a nature as to create a clear and present danger that they will bring about the substantive evils that Congress has a right to prevent. It is a question of proximity and degree. When a nation is at war many things that might be said in time of peace are such a hindrance to its effort that their utterance will not be endured so long as men fight and that no Court could regard them as protected by any constitutional right. It seems to be admitted that if an actual obstruction of the recruiting service were proved, liability for words that produced that effect might be enforced. The statute of 1917 in section 4 . . . punishes conspiracies to obstruct as well as actual obstruction. If the act, (speaking, or circulating a paper,) its tendency and the intent with which it is done are the same, we perceive no ground for saying that success alone warrants making the act a crime. . . .

Judgments affirmed.

The Right of the State to Protect Itself

FELIX FRANKFURTER

In July 1948, eleven leaders of the Communist Party of the United States were indicted for conspiring to overthrow the U.S. government by force. A jury found the defendants guilty on October 14, 1949. The Communists appealed, arguing that the First Amendment guaranteed an unlimited right to free speech and that the Declaration of Independence recognized the right of free people to revolt against their governments. The Supreme Court heard the appeal and handed down its decision in *Dennis v. United States* on June 4, 1951. By a 6-2 vote, the Court upheld the convictions. Writing for the majority, Chief Justice Frederick M. Vinson dismissed the suggestion that the right of free speech is unlimited. "Speech is not an absolute, above and beyond control by the legislature," he declared. The Court also rejected the idea that citizens enjoy a right to revolution. "Whatever theoretical merit there may be to the argument that there is a 'right' to rebellion against dictatorial governments is without force where the existing structure of the government provides for peaceful and orderly change," Vinson wrote. "We reject any principle of governmental helplessness in the face of preparation for revolution, which principle, carried to its logical conclusion, must lead to anarchy."

In his concurring opinion, Justice Felix Frankfurter cautions against taking the language of the First Amendment at face value. Instead, he calls for an interpretation of the Constitution as a living document that derives its meaning from historical circumstances. He surveys earlier Supreme Court decisions that shaped the meaning of the First Amendment and attempts to create a contemporary context for weighing its values in light of the facts of *Dennis*. In doing so, Frankfurter eloquently rebuts the notion that the First Amend-

Felix Frankfurter, opinion, *Dennis v. United States*, 341 U.S. 494, 1951.

ment is "self-defining and self-enforcing."

Frankfurter was born in Vienna, Austria, in 1882. He immigrated to the United States as a boy and received his law degree from Harvard Law School in 1906. He served as assistant U.S. attorney from 1906 to 1910 and as a legal officer in the Bureau of Insular Affairs from 1911 to 1914. He became a professor at Harvard Law School in 1914 where he taught for twenty-five years. One of the founders of the American Civil Liberties Union, Frankfurter was appointed to the Supreme Court by President Franklin Roosevelt in 1939. On the bench, Frankfurter advocated judicial restraint, believing that elected representatives were uniquely suited to determine public policy. He was the author of several books, including *The Public and Its Government* (1930), *The Commerce Clause Under Marshall, Taney, and Waite* (1937), and *Of Law and Men* (1956). He served on the Supreme Court until 1962 and died in 1965.

The defendants were convicted under [section] 3 of the Smith Act for conspiring to violate [section] 2 of that Act, which makes it unlawful "to organize or help to organize any society, group, or assembly of persons who teach, advocate, or encourage the overthrow or destruction of any government in the United States by force or violence."... The substance of the indictment is that the defendants between April 1, 1945, and July 20, 1948, agreed to bring about the dissolution of a body known as the Communist Political Association and to organize in its place the Communist Party of the United States; that the aim of the new party was "the overthrow and destruction of the Government of the United States by force and violence"; that the defendants were to assume leadership of the Party and to recruit members for it and that the Party was to publish books and conduct classes, teaching the duty and the necessity of forceful overthrow. The jury found all the defendants guilty. With one exception, each was sentenced to imprisonment for five years and to a fine of $10,000. The convictions were affirmed by the Court of Appeals for the Second Circuit. We were asked to review this affirmance on all the grounds considered by the Court of Appeals. These included not only the scope of the freedom of speech guaranteed by the Constitution, but also serious questions regarding the legal composition of the jury and the fair conduct of the trial. We granted certiorari, strictly limited, however, to the contention that 2 and 3 of the Smith Act, inherently and as applied, violated the First and Fifth Amendments. . . .

On the basis of the [judge's] instructions, the jury found, for the purpose of our review, that the advocacy which the defendants conspired to promote was to be a rule of action, by language reasonably calculated to incite persons to such action, and was intended to cause the overthrow of the Government by force and violence as soon as circumstances permit. This brings us to the ultimate issue. In enacting a statute which makes it a crime for the defendants to conspire to do what they have been found to have conspired to do, did Congress exceed its constitutional power?

Few questions of comparable import have come before this Court in recent years. The appellants maintain that they have a right to advocate a political theory, so long, at least, as their advocacy does not create an immediate danger of obvious magnitude to the very existence of our present scheme of society. On the other hand, the Government asserts the right to safeguard the security of the Nation by such a measure as the Smith Act. Our judgment is thus solicited on a conflict of interests of the utmost concern to the well-being of the country. . . .

There come occasions in law, as elsewhere, when the familiar needs to be recalled. Our whole history proves even more decisively than the course of decisions in this Court that the United States has the powers inseparable from a sovereign nation. "America has chosen to be, in many respects, and to many purposes, a nation; and for all these purposes, her government is complete; to all these objects, it is competent.". . . The right of a government to maintain its existence—self-preservation—is the most pervasive aspect of sovereignty. "Security against foreign danger," wrote [James] Madison, "is one of the primitive objects of civil society.". . . The constitutional power to act upon this basic principle has been recognized by this Court at

ility for adjusting the interests which com-
n before us of necessity belongs to the Con-
of the power to be exercised by this Court
d in decisions not charged with the emo-
tuations such as that now before us. We are
gment of those whose duty it is to legislate
reasonable basis for it. . . . We are to deter-
tute is sufficiently definite to meet the con-
ents of due process, and whether it respects
st undue concentration of authority secured
ower. . . . We must assure fairness of proce-
cope to governmental discretion but mind-
individuals in the context of the problem
course, the proceedings in a particular case
the warrant of substantial proof. Beyond
ust not go; we must scrupulously observe
judicial authority even though self-restraint
. Above all we must remember that this
udicial review is not "an exercise of the
egislature." . . .

this distribution of responsibility would
ioned. . . . But in recent decisions we have
has long been implicitly recognized. In re-
ch restrict freedoms protected by the First
ve emphasized the close relation which
to maintenance of a free society. . . . Some
rt—and at times a majority—have done
ggested that our function in reviewing
eedom of expression differs sharply from
sitting in judgment on legislation. It has
tatutes "must be justified by clear public
t doubtfully or remotely, but by clear and
ational connection between the remedy
l to be curbed, which in other contexts
lation against attack on due process
ce." . . . It has been suggested . . . that such

different periods and under diverse circumstances. "To preserve
its independence, and give security against foreign aggression
and encroachment, is the highest duty of every nation, and to
attain these ends nearly all other considerations are to be sub-
ordinated. It matters not in what form such aggression and encroachment come. . . . The government, possessing the powers
which are to be exercised for protection and security, is clothed
with authority to determine the occasion on which the powers shall be called forth. . . ." The most tragic experience in our
history [the Civil War] is a poignant reminder that the Nation's
continued existence may be threatened from within. To protect itself from such threats, the Federal Government "is in-
vested with all those inherent and implied powers which, at the
time of adopting the Constitution, were generally considered
to belong to every government as such, and as being essential
to the exercise of its functions." . . .

But even the all-embracing power and duty of self-
preservation are not absolute. Like the war power, which is indeed an aspect of the power of self-preservation, it is subject to
applicable constitutional limitations. . . . Our Constitution has
no provision lifting restrictions upon governmental authority
during periods of emergency, although the scope of a restriction may depend on the circumstances in which it is invoked.

The First Amendment is such a restriction. It exacts obedience even during periods of war; it is applicable when war
clouds are not figments of the imagination no less than when
they are. The First Amendment categorically demands that
"Congress shall make no law respecting an establishment of
religion, or prohibiting the free exercise thereof; or abridging
the freedom of speech, or of the press; or the right of the
people peaceably to assemble, and to petition the Government
for a redress of grievances." The right of a man to think what
he pleases, to write what he thinks, and to have his thoughts
made available for others to hear or read has an engaging ring
of universality. The Smith Act and this conviction under it no
doubt restrict the exercise of free speech and assembly. Does
that, without more, dispose of the matter?

AGAINST LITERAL INTERPRETATION

Just as there are those who regard as invulnerable every measure for which the claim of national survival is invoked, there are those who find in the Constitution a wholly unfettered right of expression. Such literalness treats the words of the Constitution as though they were found on a piece of outworn parchment instead of being words that have called into being a nation with a past to be preserved for the future. The soil in which the Bill of Rights grew was not a soil of arid pedantry. The historic antecedents of the First Amendment preclude the notion that its purpose was to give unqualified immunity to every expression that touched on matters within the range of political interest. The Massachusetts Constitution of 1780 guaranteed free speech; yet there are records of at least three convictions for political libels obtained between 1799 and 1803. The Pennsylvania Constitution of 1790 and the Delaware Constitution of 1792 expressly imposed liability for abuse of the right of free speech. Madison's own State put on its books in 1792 a statute confining the abusive exercise of the right of utterance. And it deserves to be noted that in writing to John Adams's wife, Jefferson did not rest his condemnation of the Sedition Act of 1798 on his belief in unrestrained utterance as to political matter. The First Amendment, he argued, reflected a limitation upon Federal power, leaving the right to enforce restrictions on speech to the States.

The language of the First Amendment is to be read not as barren words found in a dictionary but as symbols of historic experience illumined by the presuppositions of those who employed them. Not what words did Madison and [Alexander] Hamilton use, but what was it in their minds which they conveyed [their conception of government in the *Federalist* papers]? Free speech is subject to prohibition of those abuses of expression which a civilized society may forbid. As in the case of every other provision of the Constitution that is not crystallized by the nature of its technical concepts, the fact that the First Amendment is not self-defining and self-enforcing neither impairs its usefulness nor compels its paralysis as a living instrument.

legislation is not presumptively valid, ... and it has been weightily reiterated that freedom of speech has a "preferred position" among constitutional safeguards.

The precise meaning intended to be conveyed by these phrases need not now be pursued. It is enough to note that they have recurred in the Court's opinions, and their cumulative force has, not without justification, engendered belief that there is a constitutional principle, expressed by those attractive but imprecise words, prohibiting restriction upon utterance unless it creates a situation of "imminent" peril against which legislation may guard. It is on this body of the Court's pronouncements that the defendants' argument here is based.

In all fairness, the argument cannot be met by reinterpreting the Court's frequent use of "clear" and "present" to mean an entertainable "probability." In giving this meaning to the phrase "clear and present danger," the Court of Appeals was fastidiously confining the rhetoric of opinions to the exact scope of what was decided by them. We have greater responsibility for having given constitutional support, over repeated protests, to uncritical libertarian generalities.

Nor is the argument of the defendants adequately met by citing isolated cases. Adjustment of clash of interests which are at once subtle and fundamental is not likely to reveal entire consistency in a series of instances presenting the clash. It is not too difficult to find what one seeks in the language of decisions reporting the effort to reconcile free speech with the interests with which it conflicts. The case for the defendants requires that their conviction be tested against the entire body of our relevant decisions. Since the significance of every expression of thought derives from the circumstances evoking it, results reached rather than language employed give the vital meaning. ...

Unless we are to compromise judicial impartiality and subject these defendants to the risk of an ad hoc judgment influenced by the impregnating atmosphere of the times, the constitutionality of their conviction must be determined by principles established in cases decided in more tranquil periods. If those decisions are to be used as a guide and not as an argument, it is important to view them as a whole and to distrust the easy generalizations to which some of them lend themselves. . . .

These general considerations underlie the decision of the case before us.

On the one hand is the interest in security. The Communist Party was not designed by these defendants as an ordinary political party. For the circumstances of its organization, its aims and methods, and the relation of the defendants to its organization and aims we are concluded by the jury's verdict. The jury found that the Party rejects the basic premise of our political system—that change is to be brought about by non-violent constitutional process. The jury found that the Party advocates the theory that there is a duty and necessity to overthrow the Government by force and violence. It found that the Party entertains and promotes this view, not as a prophetic insight or as a bit of unworldly speculation, but as a program for winning adherents and as a policy to be translated into action.

In finding that the defendants violated the statute, we may not treat as established fact that the Communist Party in this country is of significant size, well-organized, well-disciplined, conditioned to embark on unlawful activity when given the command. But in determining whether application of the statute to the defendants is within the constitutional powers of Congress, we are not limited to the facts found by the jury. We must view such a question in the light of whatever is relevant to a legislative judgment. We may take judicial notice that the Communist doctrines which these defendants have conspired to advocate are in the ascendency in powerful nations who cannot be acquitted of unfriendliness to the institutions of this country. We may take account of evidence brought forward at this trial and elsewhere, much of which has long been common knowledge. In sum, it would amply justify a legislature in concluding that recruitment of additional members for the Party would create a substantial danger to national security.

In 1947, it has been reliably reported, at least 60,000 members were enrolled in the Party. Evidence was introduced in this case that the membership was organized in small units, linked by an intricate chain of command, and protected by elaborate precautions designed to prevent disclosure of individual identity. There are no reliable data tracing acts of sabotage or espionage directly to these defendants. But a Canadian Royal Commission appointed in 1946 to investigate espionage reported that it was "overwhelmingly established" that "the Communist movement was the principal base within which the espionage network was recruited." The most notorious spy in recent history was led into the service of the Soviet Union through Communist indoctrination. Evidence supports the conclusion that members of the Party seek and occupy positions of importance in political and labor organizations. Congress was not barred by the Constitution from believing that indifference to such experience would be an exercise not of freedom but of irresponsibility.

WHERE TO STRIKE A BALANCE

On the other hand is the interest in free speech. The right to exert all governmental powers in aid of maintaining our institutions and resisting their physical overthrow does not include intolerance of opinions and speech that cannot do harm although opposed and perhaps alien to dominant, traditional opinion. The treatment of its minorities, especially their legal position, is among the most searching tests of the level of civilization attained by a society. It is better for those who have almost unlimited power of government in their hands to err on the side of freedom. We have enjoyed so much freedom for so long that we are perhaps in danger of forgetting how much blood it cost to establish the Bill of Rights.

Of course no government can recognize a "right" of revolution, or a "right" to incite revolution if the incitement has no other purpose or effect. But speech is seldom restricted to a single purpose, and its effects may be manifold. A public interest is not wanting in granting freedom to speak their minds even to those who advocate the overthrow of the Government by force. For, as the evidence in this case abundantly illustrates, coupled with such advocacy is criticism of defects in our society. Criticism is the spur to reform; and Burke's admonition that a healthy society must reform in order to conserve has not lost its force. Astute observers have remarked that one of the characteristics of the American Republic is indifference to fundamental criticism. . . . It is a commonplace that there may be a grain of truth in the most uncouth doctrine, however false and repellent the balance may be. Suppressing advocates of overthrow inevitably will also silence critics who do not advocate overthrow but fear that their criticism may be so construed. No matter how clear we may be that the defendants now before us are preparing to overthrow our Government at the propitious moment, it is self-delusion to think that we can punish them for their advocacy without adding to the risks run by loyal citizens who honestly believe in some of the reforms these defendants advance. It is a sobering fact that in sustaining the convictions before us we can hardly escape restriction on the interchange of ideas.

We must not overlook the value of that interchange. Freedom of expression is the well-spring of our civilization—the civilization we seek to maintain and further by recognizing the right of Congress to put some limitation upon expression. Such are the paradoxes of life. For social development of trial and error, the fullest possible opportunity for the free play of the human mind is an indispensable prerequisite. The history of civilization is in considerable measure the displacement of error which once held sway as official truth by beliefs which in turn have yielded to other truths. Therefore the liberty of man to search for truth ought not to be fettered, no matter what orthodoxies he may challenge. Liberty of thought soon shrivels without freedom of expression. Nor can truth be pursued in an atmosphere hostile to the endeavor or under dangers which are hazarded only by heroes. . . .

It is not for us to decide how we would adjust the clash of interests which this case presents were the primary responsibility for reconciling it ours. Congress has determined that the danger created by advocacy of overthrow justifies the ensuing restriction on freedom of speech. The determination was made after due deliberation, and the seriousness of the congressional purpose is attested by the volume of legislation passed to effectuate the same ends.

Can we then say that the judgment Congress exercised was denied it by the Constitution? Can we establish a constitutional doctrine which forbids the elected representatives of the people to make this choice? Can we hold that the First Amendment deprives Congress of what it deemed necessary for the Government's protection? . . .

THE COURT DOES NOT DECIDE POLICY

In the light of their experience, the Framers of the Constitution chose to keep the judiciary dissociated from direct participation in the legislative process. In asserting the power to pass on the constitutionality of legislation, [Chief Justice John] Marshall and his Court [i.e. the first Supreme Court] expressed the purposes of the Founders. . . . But the extent to which the exercise of this power would interpenetrate matters of policy could hardly have been foreseen by the most prescient. The distinction which the Founders drew between the Court's duty to pass on the power of Congress and its complementary duty not to enter directly the domain of policy is fundamental. But in its actual operation it is rather subtle, certainly to the common understanding. Our duty to abstain from confounding policy with constitutionality demands perceptive humility as well as self-restraint in not declaring unconstitutional what in a judge's private judgment is deemed unwise and even dangerous.

Even when moving strictly within the limits of constitutional adjudication, judges are concerned with issues that may be said to involve vital finalities. The too easy transition from disapproval of what is undesirable to condemnation as unconstitutional, has led some of the wisest judges to question the wisdom of our scheme in lodging such authority in courts. But it is relevant to remind that in sustaining the power of Congress in a case like this nothing irrevocable is done. The democratic process at all events is not impaired or restricted.

Power and responsibility remain with the people and immediately with their representatives. All the Court says is that Congress was not forbidden by the Constitution to pass this enactment and that a prosecution under it may be brought against a conspiracy such as the one before us....

Civil liberties draw at best only limited strength from legal guaranties. Preoccupation by our people with the constitutionality, instead of with the wisdom, of legislation or of executive action is preoccupation with a false value. Even those who would most freely use the judicial brake on the democratic process by invalidating legislation that goes deeply against their grain, acknowledge, at least by paying lip service, that constitutionality does not exact a sense of proportion or the sanity of humor or an absence of fear. Focusing attention on constitutionality tends to make constitutionality synonymous with wisdom. When legislation touches freedom of thought and freedom of speech, such a tendency is a formidable enemy of the free spirit. Much that should be rejected as illiberal, because repressive and envenoming, may well be not unconstitutional. The ultimate reliance for the deepest needs of civilization must be found outside their vindication in courts of law; apart from all else, judges, howsoever they may conscientiously seek to discipline themselves against it, unconsciously are too apt to be moved by the deep undercurrents of public feeling. A persistent, positive translation of the liberating faith into the feelings and thoughts and actions of men and women is the real protection against attempts to strait-jacket the human mind. Such temptations will have their way, if fear and hatred are not exorcized. The mark of a truly civilized man is confidence in the strength and security derived from the inquiring mind. We may be grateful for such honest comforts as it supports, but we must be unafraid of its incertitudes. Without open minds there can be no open society. And if society be not open the spirit of man is mutilated and becomes enslaved.

Restricting Pornography Violates the First Amendment

WILLIAM O. DOUGLAS

On April 22, 1957, the case against publisher and bookseller Samuel Roth was brought before the U.S. Supreme Court. Roth had been convicted on four counts of violating a federal law that made punishable the mailing of material deemed "obscene, lewd, lascivious, or filthy...or other publication of an indecent character." Roth's attorneys argued that the conviction violated the First Amendment. The Court upheld the conviction, declaring that "obscenity is not within the area of constitutionally protected speech or press."

In a strongly worded dissent, Justice William O. Douglas, a member of the Court at the time, challenged the validity of the Court's finding, arguing that restrictions against pornography amount to "community censorship at its worst."

Born in Maine, Minnesota, in 1898, William O. Douglas received his law degree from Columbia in 1925 and later taught law at Yale University. As the chairman of the Securities and Exchange Commission, Douglas earned a reputation as a reformer and strong supporter of the New Deal. President Franklin Delano Roosevelt appointed Douglas to the Supreme Court in 1939. He became known on the Court for his support of civil rights and civil liberties. While serving on the Supreme Court, Douglas wrote several books, including *We the Judges* (1956) and *A Living Bill of Rights* (1961). He retired from the Court in 1975 and died five years later.

William O. Douglas, opinion, *Roth v. United States*, 354 U.S. 476, 1957.

When we sustain these convictions, we make the legality of a publication turn on the purity of thought which a book or tract instills in the mind of the reader. I do not think we can approve that standard and be faithful to the command of the First Amendment, which by its terms is a restraint on Congress and which by the Fourteenth is a restraint on the States.

In the Roth case the trial judge charged the jury that the statutory words "obscene, lewd and lascivious" describe "that form of immorality which has relation to sexual impurity and has a tendency to excite lustful thoughts." He stated that the term "filthy" in the statute pertains "to that sort of treatment of sexual matters in such a vulgar and indecent way, so that it tends to arouse a feeling of disgust and revulsion." He went on to say that the material "must be calculated to corrupt and debauch the minds and morals" of "the average person in the community," not those of any particular class. "You judge the circulars, pictures and publications which have been put in evidence by present-day standards of the community. You may ask yourselves does it offend the common conscience of the community by present-day standards."

No Clear Test of Obscenity

The trial judge who, sitting without a jury, heard the *Alberts* case and the appellate court that sustained the judgment of conviction, took California's definition of "obscenity" from *People v. Wepplo.* . . . That case held that a book is obscene "if it has a substantial tendency to deprave or corrupt its readers by inciting lascivious thoughts or arousing lustful desire."

By these standards punishment is inflicted for thoughts provoked, not for overt acts nor antisocial conduct. This test cannot be squared with our decisions under the First Amendment. Even the ill-starred *Dennis* case conceded that speech to be punishable must have some relation to action which could be penalized by government. . . . This issue cannot be avoided by saying that obscenity is not protected by the First Amendment. The question remains, what is the constitutional test of obscenity?

The tests by which these convictions were obtained require only the arousing of sexual thoughts. Yet the arousing of sexual thoughts and desires happens every day in normal life in dozens of ways. Nearly 30 years ago a questionnaire sent to college and normal school women graduates asked what things were most stimulating sexually. Of 409 replies, 9 said "music"; 18 said "pictures"; 29 said "dancing"; 40 said "drama"; 95 said "books"; and 218 said "man."

The test of obscenity the Court endorses today gives the censor free range over a vast domain. To allow the State to step in and punish mere speech or publication that the judge or the jury thinks has an undesirable impact on thoughts but that is not shown to be a part of unlawful action is drastically to curtail the First Amendment. As recently stated by two of our outstanding authorities on obscenity, "The danger of influencing a change in the current moral standards of the community, or of shocking or offending readers, or of stimulating sex thoughts or desires apart from objective conduct, can never justify the losses to society that result from interference with literary freedom.". . .

If we were certain that impurity of sexual thoughts impelled to action, we would be on less dangerous ground in punishing the distributors of this sex literature. But it is by no means clear that obscene literature, as so defined, is a significant factor in influencing substantial deviations from the community standards. . . .

RELYING ON COMMUNITY STANDARDS

The absence of dependable information on the effect of obscene literature on human conduct should make us wary. It should put us on the side of protecting society's interest in literature, except and unless it can be said that the particular publication has an impact on action that the government can control.

As noted, the trial judge in the Roth case charged the jury in the alternative that the federal obscenity statute outlaws literature dealing with sex which offends "the common conscience of the community." That standard is, in my view, more inimical still to freedom of expression.

The standard of what offends "the common conscience of the community" conflicts, in my judgment, with the command of the First Amendment that "Congress shall make no law . . . abridging the freedom of speech, or of the press." Certainly that standard would not be an acceptable one if religion, economics, politics or philosophy were involved. How does it be-

---

Roth v. United States

William Brennan Jr. served as a justice of the United States Supreme Court from 1956 to 1990.

In this excerpt from the majority opinion in Roth v. United States, *Brennan points out that obscene speech does not serve the democratic purposes the First Amendment was intended to protect.*

The primary constitutional question is whether the federal obscenity statute violates the provision of the First Amendment that "Congress shall make no law . . . abridging the freedom of speech, or of the press. . . ."

Although this is the first time the question has been squarely presented to this Court, . . . expressions found in numerous opinions indicate that this Court has always assumed that obscenity is not protected by the freedoms of speech and press. . . .

The guaranties of freedom of expression in effect in 10 of the 14 States which by 1792 had ratified the Constitution, gave no absolute protection for every utterance. Thirteen of the 14 States provided for the prosecution of libel, and all of those States made either blasphemy or profanity, or both, statutory crimes. . . .

In light of this history, it is apparent that the uncondi-

come a constitutional standard when literature treating with sex is concerned?

Any test that turns on what is offensive to the community's standards is too loose, too capricious, too destructive of freedom of expression to be squared with the First Amendment. Under that test, juries can censor, suppress, and punish what they don't like, provided the matter relates to "sexual impurity" or has a tendency "to excite lustful thoughts." This is

tional phrasing of the First Amendment was not intended to protect every utterance. This phrasing did not prevent this Court from concluding that libelous utterances are not within the area of constitutionally protected speech. At the time of the adoption of the First Amendment, obscenity law was not as fully developed as libel law, but there is sufficiently contemporaneous evidence to show that obscenity, too, was outside the protection intended for speech and press.

The protection given speech and press was fashioned to assure unfettered interchange of ideas for the bringing about of political and social changes desired by the people. . . .

All ideas having even the slightest redeeming social importance—unorthodox ideas, controversial ideas, even ideas hateful to the prevailing climate of opinion—have the full protection of the guaranties, unless excludable because they encroach upon the limited area of more important interests. But implicit in the history of the First Amendment is the rejection of obscenity as utterly without redeeming social importance. . . .

We hold that obscenity is not within the area of constitutionally protected speech or press.

U.S. Supreme Court, *Roth v. United States*, 354 U.S. 476, 1957.

community censorship in one of its worst forms. It creates a regime where in the battle between the literati and the Philistines, the Philistines are certain to win. If experience in this field teaches anything, it is that "censorship of obscenity has almost always been both irrational and indiscriminate.". . . The test adopted here accentuates that trend. . . .

I can understand (and at times even sympathize) with programs of civic groups and church groups to protect and defend the existing moral standards of the community. I can understand the motives of the Anthony Comstocks who would impose Victorian standards on the community. When speech alone is involved, I do not think that government, consistently with the First Amendment, can become the sponsor of any of these movements. I do not think that government, consistently with the First Amendment, can throw its weight behind one school or another. Government should be concerned with antisocial conduct, not with utterances. Thus, if the First Amendment guarantee of freedom of speech and press is to mean anything in this field, it must allow protests even against the moral code that the standard of the day sets for the community. In other words, literature should not be suppressed merely because it offends the moral code of the censor.

The legality of a publication in this country should never be allowed to turn either on the purity of thought which it instills in the mind of the reader or on the degree to which it offends the community conscience. By either test the role of the censor is exalted, and society's values in literary freedom are sacrificed.

WRONGFULLY ASSESSING THE VALUE OF SPEECH

The Court today suggests a third standard. It defines obscene material as that "which deals with sex in a manner appealing to prurient interest." Like the standards applied by the trial judges below, that standard does not require any nexus between the literature which is prohibited and action which the legislature can regulate or prohibit. Under the First Amendment, that standard is no more valid than those which the courts below adopted.

I do not think that the problem can be resolved by the Court's statement that "obscenity is not expression protected by the First Amendment." With the exception of *Beauharnais v. Illinois*, none of our cases has resolved problems of free speech and free press by placing any form of expression beyond the pale of the absolute prohibition of the First Amendment. Unlike the law of libel, wrongfully relied on in *Beauharnais*, there is no special historical evidence that literature dealing with sex was intended to be treated in a special manner by those who drafted the First Amendment. In fact, the first reported court decision in this country involving obscene literature was in 1821.... I reject too the implication that problems of freedom of speech and of the press are to be resolved by weighing against the values of free expression, the judgment of the Court that a particular form of that expression has "no redeeming social importance." The First Amendment, its prohibition in terms absolute, was designed to preclude courts as well as legislatures from weighing the values of speech against silence. The First Amendment puts free speech in the preferred position.

Freedom of expression can be suppressed if, and to the extent that, it is so closely brigaded with illegal action as to be an inseparable part of it.... As a people, we cannot afford to relax that standard. For the test that suppresses a cheap tract today can suppress a literary gem tomorrow. All it need do is to incite a lascivious thought or arouse a lustful desire. The list of books that judges or juries can place in that category is endless.

I would give the broad sweep of the First Amendment full support. I have the same confidence in the ability of our people to reject noxious literature as I have in their capacity to sort out the true from the false in theology, economics, politics, or any other field.

Offensive Speech Is Protected by the First Amendment

WILLIAM BRENNAN JR.

In 1984 Revolutionary Communist Party member Gregory Johnson protested the Republican National Convention in Dallas by burning an American flag. Johnson was arrested and convicted under Texas flag desecration law. In 1989 the U.S. Supreme Court overturned Johnson's conviction and struck down the Texas law against flag desecration. The Court reasoned that, because the burning of the flag made a political statement, it qualified as "expressive conduct protected by the First Amendment." Justice William Brennan Jr. wrote the majority opinion in which he asserted, "If there is a bedrock principle underlying the First Amendment, it is that the government may not prohibit the expression of an idea simply because society finds the idea itself offensive or disagreeable."

The second of eight children born to Irish immigrants, William Brennan Jr. was born on April 25, 1906 in Newark, New Jersey. After graduating from the University of Pennsylvania, he attended Harvard Law School, receiving his law degree in 1931. Later that year, he returned to Newark to open a law office. During World War II, he served as an army Judge Advocate General (JAG) officer. He became a superior court judge in 1949, then moved up to the appellate division in 1950. He was appointed to the New Jersey Supreme Court in 1952. Four years later President Dwight D. Eisenhower named Brennan to the U.S. Supreme Court. A champion of individual liberties and an opponent of the death penalty, Brennan served on the Court from 1956 to 1990 and wrote more than thirteen hundred opinions. He died on July 24, 1997.

William Brennan Jr., opinion, *Texas v. Johnson*, 491 U.S. 397, 1989.

After publicly burning an American flag as a means of political protest, Gregory Lee Johnson was convicted of desecrating a flag in violation of Texas law. This case presents the question whether his conviction is consistent with the First Amendment. We hold that it is not.

THE OFFENSE

While the Republican National Convention was taking place in Dallas in 1984, respondent Johnson participated in a political demonstration dubbed the "Republican War Chest Tour." As explained in literature distributed by the demonstrators and in speeches made by them, the purpose of this event was to protest the policies of the [Ronald] Reagan administration and of certain Dallas-based corporations. The demonstrators marched through the Dallas streets, chanting political slogans and stopping at several corporate locations to stage "die-ins" intended to dramatize the consequences of nuclear war. On several occasions they spray-painted the walls of buildings and overturned potted plants, but Johnson himself took no part in such activities. He did, however, accept an American flag handed to him by a fellow protestor who had taken it from a flagpole outside one of the targeted buildings.

The demonstration ended in front of Dallas City Hall, where Johnson unfurled the American flag, doused it with kerosene, and set it on fire. While the flag burned, the protestors chanted: "America, the red, white, and blue, we spit on you." After the demonstrators dispersed, a witness to the flag burning collected the flag's remains and buried them in his backyard. No one was physically injured or threatened with injury, though several witnesses testified that they had been seriously offended by the flag burning.

Of the approximately 100 demonstrators, Johnson alone was charged with a crime. The only criminal offense with which he was charged was the desecration of a venerated object in violation of Tex. Penal Code Ann. 42.09(a)(3) (1989). After a trial, he was convicted, sentenced to one year in prison, and fined $2,000. The Court of Appeals for the Fifth District of Texas at Dallas affirmed Johnson's conviction, . . . but the Texas Court of Criminal Appeals reversed, . . . holding that the State could not, consistent with the First Amendment, punish Johnson for burning the flag in these circumstances.

RECOGNIZING SYMBOLIC SPEECH

The Court of Criminal Appeals began by recognizing that Johnson's conduct was symbolic speech protected by the First Amendment: "Given the context of an organized demonstration, speeches, slogans, and the distribution of literature, anyone who observed appellant's act would have understood the message that appellant intended to convey. The act for which appellant was convicted was clearly 'speech' contemplated by the First Amendment.". . . To justify Johnson's conviction for engaging in symbolic speech, the State asserted two interests: preserving the flag as a symbol of national unity and preventing breaches of the peace. The Court of Criminal Appeals held that neither interest supported his conviction. . . .

We granted certiorari, (1988), and now affirm. . . .

The First Amendment literally forbids the abridgment only of "speech," but we have long recognized that its protection does not end at the spoken or written word. . . .

Especially pertinent to this case are our decisions recognizing the communicative nature of conduct relating to flags. Attaching a peace sign to the flag . . . ; refusing to salute the flag . . . ; and displaying a red flag . . . , we have held, all may find shelter under the First Amendment. . . . That we have had little difficulty identifying an expressive element in conduct relating to flags should not be surprising. The very purpose of a national flag is to serve as a symbol of our country; it is, one might say, "the one visible manifestation of two hundred years of nationhood." Thus, we have observed:

> The flag salute is a form of utterance. Symbolism is a primitive but effective way of communicating ideas. The use of an emblem or flag to symbolize some system, idea, institution, or personality, is a short cut from mind to mind. Causes and nations, political parties, lodges and ecclesiastical groups

seek to knit the loyalty of their followings to a flag or banner, a color or design. . . .

Pregnant with expressive content, the flag as readily signifies this Nation as does the combination of letters found in "America."

CONSIDERING CONTEXT

We have not automatically concluded, however, that any action taken with respect to our flag is expressive. Instead, in characterizing such action for First Amendment purposes, we have considered the context in which it occurred. In [*Spence v. Washington* (1974)], for example, we emphasized that Spence's taping of a peace sign to his flag was "roughly simultaneous with and concededly triggered by the Cambodian incursion and the Kent State tragedy." The State of Washington had conceded, in fact, that Spence's conduct was a form of communication, and we stated that "the State's concession is inevitable on this record."

The State of Texas conceded for purposes of its oral argument in this case that Johnson's conduct was expressive conduct, . . . and this concession seems to us as prudent as was Washington's in *Spence*. Johnson burned an American flag as part—indeed, as the culmination—of a political demonstration that coincided with the convening of the Republican Party and its renomination of Ronald Reagan for President. The expressive, overtly political nature of this conduct was both intentional and overwhelmingly apparent. At his trial, Johnson explained his reasons for burning the flag as follows: "The American Flag was burned as Ronald Reagan was being renominated as President. And a more powerful statement of symbolic speech, whether you agree with it or not, couldn't have been made at that time. It's quite a just position [juxtaposition]. We had new patriotism and no patriotism.". . . In these circumstances, Johnson's burning of the flag was conduct "sufficiently imbued with elements of communication," . . . to implicate the First Amendment.

The government generally has a freer hand in restricting expressive conduct than it has in restricting the written or spoken word. . . . It may not, however, proscribe particular conduct because it has expressive elements. . . . "A law directed at the communicative nature of conduct must, like a law directed at speech itself, be justified by the substantial showing of need that the First Amendment requires.". . . It is, in short, not simply the verbal or nonverbal nature of the expression, but the governmental interest at stake, that helps to determine whether a restriction on that expression is valid. . . .

We must decide whether Texas has asserted an interest in support of Johnson's conviction that is unrelated to the suppression of expression. . . . The State offers two separate interests to justify this conviction: preventing breaches of the peace and preserving the flag as a symbol of nationhood and national unity. We hold that the first interest is not implicated on this record and that the second is related to the suppression of expression. . . .

BREACH OF THE PEACE

Texas claims that its interest in preventing breaches of the peace justifies Johnson's conviction for flag desecration. However, no disturbance of the peace actually occurred or threatened to occur because of Johnson's burning of the flag. Although the State stresses the disruptive behavior of the protestors during their march toward City Hall, . . . it admits that "no actual breach of the peace occurred at the time of the flagburning or in response to the flagburning." The State's emphasis on the protestors' disorderly actions prior to arriving at City Hall is not only somewhat surprising given that no charges were brought on the basis of this conduct, but it also fails to show that a disturbance of the peace was a likely reaction to Johnson's conduct. The only evidence offered by the State at trial to show the reaction to Johnson's actions was the testimony of several persons who had been seriously offended by the flag burning. . . .

The State's position, therefore, amounts to a claim that an audience that takes serious offense at particular expression is necessarily likely to disturb the peace and that the expression may be prohibited on this basis. Our precedents do not countenance such a presumption. On the contrary, they recognize that a principal "function of free speech under our system of government is to invite dispute. It may indeed best serve its high purpose when it induces a condition of unrest, creates dissatisfaction with conditions as they are, or even stirs people to anger." *Terminiello v. Chicago*, (1949). . . .

Thus, we have not permitted the government to assume that every expression of a provocative idea will incite a riot, but have instead required careful consideration of the actual circumstances surrounding such expression, asking whether the expression "is directed to inciting or producing imminent lawless action and is likely to incite or produce such action." *Brandenburg v. Ohio*, (1969). . . .

Nor does Johnson's expressive conduct fall within that small class of "fighting words" that are "likely to provoke the average person to retaliation, and thereby cause a breach of the peace." *Chaplinsky v. New Hampshire*, (1942). No reasonable onlooker would have regarded Johnson's generalized expression of dissatisfaction with the policies of the Federal Government as a direct personal insult or an invitation to exchange fisticuffs. . . .

We thus conclude that the State's interest in maintaining order is not implicated on these facts. The State need not worry that our holding will disable it from preserving the peace. We do not suggest that the First Amendment forbids a State to prevent "imminent lawless action.". . . And, in fact, Texas already has a statute specifically prohibiting breaches of the peace, . . . which tends to confirm that Texas need not punish this flag desecration in order to keep the peace. . . .

PRESERVING A NATIONAL SYMBOL

The State also asserts an interest in preserving the flag as a symbol of nationhood and national unity. In *Spence*, we acknowledged that the government's interest in preserving the flag's special symbolic value "is directly related to expression in the context of activity" such as affixing a peace symbol to a flag. We are equally persuaded that this interest is related to expression in the case of Johnson's burning of the flag. . . .

It remains to consider whether the State's interest in preserving the flag as a symbol of nationhood and national unity justifies Johnson's conviction. . . .

Johnson was not . . . prosecuted for the expression of just any idea; he was prosecuted for his expression of dissatisfaction with the policies of this country, expression situated at the core of our First Amendment values. . . .

Moreover, Johnson was prosecuted because he knew that his politically charged expression would cause "serious offense." If he had burned the flag as a means of disposing of it because it was dirty or torn, he would not have been convicted of flag desecration under this Texas law: federal law designates burning as the preferred means of disposing of a flag "when it is in such condition that it is no longer a fitting emblem for display,". . . and Texas has no quarrel with this means of disposal. . . . The Texas law is thus not aimed at protecting the physical integrity of the flag in all circumstances, but is designed instead to protect it only against impairments that would cause serious offense to others. . . .

Whether Johnson's treatment of the flag violated Texas law thus depended on the likely communicative impact of his expressive conduct. Our decision in *Boos v. Barry* . . . tells us that this restriction on Johnson's expression is content based. In *Boos*, we considered the constitutionality of a law prohibiting "the display of any sign within 500 feet of a foreign embassy if that sign tends to bring that foreign government into 'public odium' or 'public disrepute.'". . . Rejecting the argument that the law was content neutral because it was justified by "our international law obligation to shield diplomats from speech that offends their dignity,". . . we held that "[t]he emotive impact of speech on its audience is not a 'secondary effect'" unrelated to the content of the expression itself. . . .

According to the principles announced in *Boos*, Johnson's political expression was restricted because of the content of the message he conveyed. We must therefore subject the State's asserted interest in preserving the special symbolic character of the flag to "the most exacting scrutiny.". . .

Texas argues that its interest in preserving the flag as a symbol of nationhood and national unity survives this close analysis. Quoting extensively from the writings of this Court chronicling the flag's historic and symbolic role in our society, the State emphasizes the "special place" reserved for the flag in our Nation. . . . The State's claim is that it has an interest in preserving the flag as a symbol of nationhood and national unity, a symbol with a determinate range of meanings. . . . According to Texas, if one physically treats the flag in a way that would tend to cast doubt on either the idea that nationhood and national unity are the flag's referents or that national unity actually exists, the message conveyed thereby is a harmful one and therefore may be prohibited.

No Precedent

If there is a bedrock principle underlying the First Amendment, it is that the government may not prohibit the expression of an idea simply because society finds the idea itself offensive or disagreeable. . . .

We have not recognized an exception to this principle even where our flag has been involved. In *Street v. New York*, (1969), we held that a State may not criminally punish a person for uttering words critical of the flag. Rejecting the argument that the conviction could be sustained on the ground that Street had "failed to show the respect for our national symbol which may properly be demanded of every citizen," we concluded that "the constitutionally guaranteed 'freedom to be intellectually . . . diverse or even contrary,' and the 'right to differ as to things that touch the heart of the existing order,' encompass the freedom to express publicly one's opinions about our flag, including those opinions which are defiant or contemptuous."
. . . Nor may the government, we have held, compel conduct that would evince respect for the flag. "To sustain the compulsory flag salute we are required to say that a Bill of Rights which guards the individual's right to speak his own mind, left it open to public authorities to compel him to utter what is not in his mind." . . .

In holding in [*West Virginia Board of Education v. Barnette* (1943)] that the Constitution did not leave this course open to the government, Justice Jackson described one of our society's defining principles in words deserving of their frequent repetition: "If there is any fixed star in our constitutional constellation, it is that no official, high or petty, can prescribe what shall be orthodox in politics, nationalism, religion, or other matters of opinion or force citizens to confess by word or act their faith therein." In *Spence*, we held that the same interest asserted by Texas here was insufficient to support a criminal conviction under a flag-misuse statute for the taping of a peace sign to an American flag. "Given the protected character of [Spence's] expression and in light of the fact that no interest the State may have in preserving the physical integrity of a privately owned flag was significantly impaired on these facts," we held, "the conviction must be invalidated.". . .

Texas' focus on the precise nature of Johnson's expression, moreover, misses the point of our prior decisions: their enduring lesson, that the government may not prohibit expression simply because it disagrees with its message, is not dependent on the particular mode in which one chooses to express an idea. If we were to hold that a State may forbid flag burning wherever it is likely to endanger the flag's symbolic role, but allow it wherever burning a flag promotes that role—as where, for example, a person ceremoniously burns a dirty flag—we would be saying that when it comes to impairing the flag's physical integrity, the flag itself may be used as a symbol—as a substitute for the written or spoken word or a "short cut from mind to mind"—only in one direction. We would be permitting a State to "prescribe what shall be orthodox" by saying that one may burn the flag to convey one's attitude toward it and its referents only if one does not endanger the flag's representation of nationhood and national unity.

A TERRITORY WITH NO BOUNDARIES

We never before have held that the Government may ensure that a symbol be used to express only one view of that symbol or its referents. Indeed, in *Schacht v. United States*, we invalidated a federal statute permitting an actor portraying a member of one of our Armed Forces to "wear the uniform of that armed force if the portrayal does not tend to discredit that armed force.". . . This proviso, we held, "which leaves Americans free to praise the war in Vietnam but can send persons like Schacht to prison for opposing it, cannot survive in a country which has the First Amendment.". . .

We perceive no basis on which to hold that the principle underlying our decision in *Schacht* does not apply to this case. To conclude that the government may permit designated symbols to be used to communicate only a limited set of messages would be to enter territory having no discernible or defensible boundaries. Could the government, on this theory, prohibit the burning of state flags? Of copies of the Presidential seal? Of the Constitution? In evaluating these choices under the First Amendment, how would we decide which symbols were sufficiently special to warrant this unique status? To do so, we would be forced to consult our own political preferences, and impose them on the citizenry, in the very way that the First Amendment forbids us to do. . . .

It is not the State's ends, but its means, to which we object. . . . We do not doubt that the government has a legitimate interest in making efforts to "preserv[e] the national flag as an unalloyed symbol of our country.". . . To say that the government has an interest in encouraging proper treatment of the flag, however, is not to say that it may criminally punish a person for burning a flag as a means of political protest. "National unity as an end which officials may foster by persuasion and example is not in question. The problem is whether under our Constitution compulsion as here employed is a permissible means for its achievement.". . .

THE COURT'S CONCLUSION

We are fortified in today's conclusion by our conviction that forbidding criminal punishment for conduct such as Johnson's will not endanger the special role played by our flag or the feelings it inspires. To paraphrase Justice Holmes, we submit that nobody can suppose that this one gesture of an unknown man will change our Nation's attitude towards its flag. . . . Indeed, Texas' argument that the burning of an American flag "is an act having a high likelihood to cause a breach of the peace,". . . and its statute's implicit assumption that physical mistreatment of the flag will lead to "serious offense," tend to confirm that the flag's special role is not in danger; if it were, no one would riot or take offense because a flag had been burned.

We are tempted to say, in fact, that the flag's deservedly cherished place in our community will be strengthened, not weakened, by our holding today. Our decision is a reaffirmation of the principles of freedom and inclusiveness that the flag best reflects, and of the conviction that our toleration of criticism such as Johnson's is a sign and source of our strength. Indeed, one of the proudest images of our flag, the one immortalized in our own national anthem, is of the bombardment it survived at Fort McHenry. It is the Nation's resilience, not its rigidity, that Texas sees reflected in the flag—and it is that resilience that we reassert today.

The way to preserve the flag's special role is not to punish those who feel differently about these matters. It is to persuade them that they are wrong. "To courageous, self-reliant men, with confidence in the power of free and fearless reasoning applied through the processes of popular government, no danger flowing from speech can be deemed clear and present, unless the incidence of the evil apprehended is so imminent that it may befall before there is opportunity for full discussion. If there be time to expose through discussion the falsehood and fallacies, to avert the evil by the processes of education, the remedy to be applied is more speech, not enforced silence." *Whitney v. California*, (1927). . . . And, precisely because it is our flag that is involved, one's response to the flag burner may exploit the uniquely persuasive power of the flag itself. We can imagine no more appropriate response to burning a flag than waving one's own, no better way to counter a flag burner's message than by saluting the flag that burns, no surer means of preserving the dignity even of the flag that burned than by—as one witness here did—according its remains a respectful burial. We do not consecrate the flag by punishing its desecration, for in doing so we dilute the freedom that this cherished emblem represents. . . .

Johnson was convicted for engaging in expressive conduct. The State's interest in preventing breaches of the peace does not support his conviction because Johnson's conduct did not threaten to disturb the peace. Nor does the State's interest in preserving the flag as a symbol of nationhood and national unity justify his criminal conviction for engaging in political expression. The judgment of the Texas Court of Criminal Appeals is therefore—Affirmed.

CHAPTER 4

FREE SPEECH AS A SOCIAL MOVEMENT

The Alien and Sedition Acts of 1798

NAT HENTOFF

Born in Boston in 1925, Nat Hentoff graduated from Northeastern University and continued his studies at Harvard. After spending a year studying at the Sorbonne in Paris as a Fulbright fellow, Hentoff returned to the United States to become an associate editor for the jazz magazine *Down Beat*. He later served as a staff writer for the *New Yorker* and a columnist for the *Washington Post*. He continues to write columns for the *Village Voice* and the *Washington Times*. In 1980, the American Bar Association honored him with its Silver Gavel Award for his coverage of the law, and in 1985 he received an honorary doctorate of law from Northeastern University. He is the author of biographies, novels, children's books, jazz books, and books about civil liberties.

In this excerpt from his 1980 book *The First Freedom: The Tumultuous History of Free Speech in America*, Hentoff recounts how the passage of the Alien and Sedition Acts of 1798 criminalized "false, scandalous, and malicious [speech] against the government of the United States," creating a constitutional crisis.

In 1798 Congress, dominated by the Federalist party, enacted the Alien and Sedition Acts, making political dissent against government policy as dangerous as if there were no First Amendment in the new republic.

The Federalists believed that the nation should be directed by an elite, people of marked talent and wealth. Their opposition, the Democratic-Republicans (of whom Thomas Jefferson was a leader), were both suspicious of centralized authority and insistent that government must be responsive to the people at large. The Republicans also saw America as a sanctuary for the oppressed and a symbol to the world of the self-governing liberty of free men.

When France declared war on Great Britain in 1793, the Republicans tended to favor the French while Federalist sympathies were with the British. As time went on, relations between the American and French governments steadily deteriorated, and war between France and the new nation seemed imminent. Adding to the rising tension at home were rumors of French espionage and of French plots against the republic, along with great outrage over French attacks on American shipping.

CONGRESS CRIMINALIZES SPEECH

With fear and anger in the land, the Federalists saw a chance to beat down their Republican opposition, including the aggressive Republican press that was continually attacking the Federalist government. Federalist Alexander Hamilton warned that many of the Republicans so fiercely opposed to the anti-French policy of President John Adams would ultimately be regarded by the people as similar to "the Tories of our Revolution." And, in 1798, the Federalists pushed the Alien and Sedition Acts through Congress.

Three of the laws were mainly directed against French and Irish immigrants, most of them Republicans. The government was empowered to arrest and deport any foreigner judged "dangerous" to the nation's peace and safety or suspected of "secret machinations." Although these provisions dealing with aliens were not enforced, many aliens, in acute apprehension, either went into hiding or fled the country.

The statute dealing with seditious speech *was* enforced, mostly against the Democratic-Republican citizens of the new nation. This act punished, by fine and imprisonment, anyone who uttered, wrote, or published "any false scandalous and malicious [speech] against the government of the United States," including the President and the Congress. It was now seditious to use speech that would bring the President or Congress "into contempt or disrepute" or that might excite against them "the hatred of the good people of the United States," thereby stirring up "sedition within the United States."

If convicted of exercising this kind of speech—which had presumably been protected by the First Amendment—the miscreant could be fined up to two thousand dollars and could be imprisoned for up to two years. As one legacy of the John Peter Zenger case,[1] however, the Sedition Act did specify the right of the accused to plead the truth of what he had said or written as a defense against the charge of seditious libel. Moreover, the jury would have the right to determine both the law and the facts of the case.

CRITICS RIDICULE THE NEW LAW

On the passage of the Sedition Act, the Republican press was understandably outraged. The *Boston Independent Chronicle*, for instance, sternly reminded its readers that in a free country it remained the *duty* of citizens to speak their minds, "and may the hand be palsied that shrinks back from its duties." The very day President John Adams signed the bill, the Philadelphia *Aurora*—the nation's leading Republican journal, edited by Benjamin Franklin Bache, grandson of Benjamin Franklin—ran this "Advertisement Extraordinary!!!":

> *Orator Mum* takes the very orderly method of announcing to his fellow citizens that a thinking Club will be established in a few days at the sign of the *Muzzle* in *Gag* street. The first subject for cogitation will be:
>
> "Ought a Free People to obey the laws which violate the constitution they have sworn to support?"
>
> N.B. No member will be permitted to think longer than fifteen minutes.

1. In 1735, a colonial jury, defying the instructions of the presiding judge, found publisher John Peter Zenger not guilty of libel based on the fact that what he had printed was true.

The wit was defiant, but those enforcing the Sedition Act were sufficiently impervious to such wit to have brought about at least twenty-five arrests, fifteen indictments, and ten convictions within the two years it was in force.

THE CASE OF MATTHEW LYON

To give a sense of the vengeful spirit of that period, there is the case of the Sedition Act's first victim, Congressman Matthew Lyon of Vermont. Born in Ireland, Lyon had come to America as an indentured servant, earned his freedom, and fought in the Revolution. Having prospered in the state of Vermont, he had published a newspaper, among his other enterprises there, from 1773 to 1775.

Among the charges leveled against Lyon under the Sedition Act was a letter he had writted to the *Vermont Journal* in Windsor in answer to a vehement attack on him by that Federalist paper. In the letter Lyon said that John Adams's administration had entirely forgotten the public welfare "in an unbounded thirst for ridiculous pomp, foolish adulation, and selfish avarice." Another alleged crime was Lyon's having quoted, during a reelection campaign, from a letter by American poet John Barlow, then in France. Barlow had wondered that Congress, in response to a "bullying speech" by President Adams, had not given "an order to send him to a mad house."

On these charges of malicious sedition, Lyon was tried, fined, and jailed. On hearing the news, Thomas Jefferson, in Virginia, wrote, "I know not which mortifies me most, that I should fear to write what I think or that my country bear such a state of things. Yet Lyon's judges . . . are objects of national fear."

In October 1798, seven years after the First Amendment's addition to the Constitution, Matthew Lyon, in punishment for expressing his ideas, was paraded through the town of Vergennes, Vermont, on his way to a twelve-by-sixteen cell, "the common receptacle for horse-thieves, money-makers, runaway-negroes, or any kind of felons." As described by historian James Morton Smith, the cell contained "an indoor toilet in one corner of the room [which] perfumed the air with a stockyardlike aroma. Light and air came through a small window, which was crossed by nine iron bars. The cell had neither fireplace nor stove." There the Revolutionary patriot remained until the following February, when a group of his constituents raised the money to pay Lyon's fine. (He had been reelected to Congress while in jail.)

Republicans throughout the new nation toasted his release, and at a Liberty Tree celebration in Bridgehampton, New York, tribute was paid to "Colonel Matthew Lyon, the martyr to the cause of Liberty and the Rights of Man: may his suffering bring good out of evil by arousing the people to guard their rights and oppose every unconstitutional measure."

Among others imprisoned under the Sedition Act were the editors of four of the five most important Republican newspapers in the country. There were less influential targets as well. A town drunk, for instance, who was on hand when President Adams came through to the accompaniment of a sixteen-gun salute, said, "I do not care if they fired through his ass." He was found guilty of contempt of the President under the Sedition Act.

"DOWNFALL TO THE TYRANTS OF AMERICA"

The prosecution that resulted in the longest prison sentence under the act took place in Dedham, Massachusetts, where a number of people had set up a Liberty Pole to which they attached a sign reading "No Stamp Act, No Sedition, No Alien Bills, No Land Tax; downfall to the Tyrants of America."

Outraged over this "outbreak of sedition" (as one Federalist paper called it), the authorities arrested and indicted two of those responsible for this criminal act of free expression. One expressed deep repentance. The spirit of the other, however, would not be broken. Nor would he name his associates in this seditious enterprise because, he told the judge, if he did so, "I would lose all my friends." Accordingly, the culprit, a veteran of the Revolutionary Army and a common laborer with little formal schooling, was convicted of having created a "rallying point of insurrection and civil war." He languished in jail for two years.

PRESIDENTIAL PARDONS

Many Republican politicians and journalists defied the Sedition Act, and popular opinion was so shocked by it that the presidential victory of Thomas Jefferson in 1800 was due in considerable part to the citizenry's abhorrence of this Federalist legislation. The Sedition Act expired on March 3, 1801; Jefferson pardoned everyone who had been convicted under it. In time Congress also repaid most of the fines.

No case under the Sedition Act ever reached the Supreme Court, but ominously, the constitutionality of the act *was* sustained by lower federal courts, including three Supreme Court Justices riding circuit (hearing cases, individually, away from Washington). Indeed, it was not until 1964 that the Supreme Court, in effect, struck down that anti–First Amendment legislation, declaring:

> Although the Sedition Act was never tested in this Court, the attack upon its validity has carried the day in the court of history. . . . [There has been] a broad consensus that the Act, because of the restraint it imposed upon criticism of government and public officials, was inconsistent with the First Amendment.

THE "GUARDIAN OF EVERY OTHER RIGHT"

Jefferson and Madison, of course, had immediately come to that conclusion when the Alien and Sedition Acts were passed. Jefferson called them an unconstitutional "reign of terror," and Madison charged that Congress's promulgation of the Alien and Sedition Acts "ought to produce universal alarm because it is levelled against the right of freely examining public characters and measures, and of free communication among the people thereon, which has ever been justly deemed *the only effectual guardian of every other right*" (emphasis added).

To insure that there could be no possible doubt as to what

the framers of the Constitution and the Bill of Rights had intended, Madison asked the fundamental question: "Is then the federal government destitute of every authority for restraining the licentiousness of the press, and for shielding itself against the libellous attacks which may be made on those who administer it?"

The clear answer is in the First Amendment. Said Madison, "The answer must be that the federal government is destitute of all such authority." The censorial power is in the people over the government, not in the government over the people. Accordingly, the Alien and Sedition Acts profoundly violate the Constitution.

The Struggle for
Free Speech in
the Civil War

MICHAEL KENT CURTIS

In this excerpt from his 2000 book *Free Speech, "The People's Darling Privilege": Struggles for Freedom of Expression in American History*, Michael Kent Curtis describes how President Abraham Lincoln's wartime proclamation establishing martial law and outlawing "any disloyal practice, affording aid and comfort to Rebels" led to the arrest, conviction, and banishment of outspoken critic Clement L. Vallandigham. Curtis describes various reactions to Vallandigham's arrest as well as Lincoln's response to criticism of his policy.

Curtis is a professor of constitutional law and history at Wake Forest University School of Law. He received a B.A. degree from the University of the South, in Sewanee, Tennessee; a law degree from University of North Carolina (Chapel Hill) School of Law; and an M.A. degree from the University of Chicago. Before joining the faculty of Wake Forest University in 1991, he spent twenty years as a partner in the law firm of Smith, Patterson, Follin, Curtis, James, Harkavy & Lawrence. In 1985 the North Carolina Civil Liberties Union presented him with the Frank Porter Graham Award for achievement in defending and advancing civil liberties in North Carolina. He is the author of three books and numerous articles on free speech and constitutional history.

A t 2:40 A.M. on May 5, 1863, 150 Union soldiers from the command of General Ambrose Burnside arrived at Clement L. Vallandigham's home in Dayton, Ohio. The soldiers' mission was to arrest Vallandigham, a prominent Dem-

Michael Kent Curtis, *Free Speech, "The People's Darling Privilege": Struggles for Freedom of Expression in American History*. Durham, NC: Duke University Press, 2000. Copyright © 2000 by Michael Kent Curtis. All rights reserved. Reproduced by permission.

ocratic politician and former congressman, for an antiwar political speech he had made a few days before at a Democratic Party rally. After Vallandigham refused to submit, the soldiers attempted to break down his front door. Finally, soldiers broke several doors and captured Vallandigham. They put him on a train for Cincinnati to be tried before a military commission, appointed by the same general who had ordered his arrest. Vallandigham's efforts to secure a writ of habeas corpus[1] failed. After his conviction, President Lincoln changed Vallandigham's sentence from imprisonment to banishment to the Confederacy.

The most immediate response to the Vallandigham arrest was a riot in his hometown. A mob burned the local Republican newspaper building and cut telegraph lines. Order was restored only when General Burnside declared martial law and sent in troops.

The arrest of Vallandigham produced a tidal wave of criticism. The arrest focused national attention on the meaning of free speech in time of war (especially civil war), on the relation of free speech to democratic government, and on civil liberties for critics of the Lincoln administration. Critics insisted the arrest violated Bill of Rights guarantees of free speech, free assembly, jury trial, due process, and right to grand jury indictment. Both Democrats and Republicans described such rights as "privileges" or "immunities" as well as "rights" and "liberties.". . .

Before the Civil War, abolitionists and, later, Republicans had invoked protective concepts of freedom of speech, press, assembly, and religion to defend against attempts to suppress antislavery expression. They claimed the right to discuss questions of public policy fully and freely on every inch of American soil "to which the privileges and immunities of the Constitution extend," as Representative [Owen] Lovejoy put it in 1860. "[T]hat Constitution," he said, "guaranties me free

---

1. A legal document issued to those seeking to be brought before a judge to begin an inquiry into an illegal abridgment of their civil rights.

speech." In response to an uproar over Republican endorsement of Hinton Helper's strongly antislavery book, Republicans in the United States Senate supported a resolution that asserted, "[F]reedom of speech and of the press on [the morality and expediency of slavery and on] and every other subject of domestic [state] and national policy, should be maintained inviolate." Republicans, abolitionists, and others described the rights to free speech and press as constitutional privileges belonging to all American citizens, rights enjoyed by virtue of the federal constitution. Antislavery activists and Republicans had implicitly and explicitly repudiated the notion that free speech or press was limited merely to a protection against prior restraints, but that punishment after publication was permissible. Instead they insisted that, by punishing antislavery speech and press, slave states refused to tolerate freedom of speech. Similarly, they implicitly and sometimes explicitly rejected arguments that the bad tendency of anti-slavery speech (a tendency that outraged Southerners and that their Northern allies had insisted threatened slave revolts and disunion) justified suppression. The Republican Party slogan in 1856 was "Free Speech, Free Press, Free Men, Free Labor, Free Territory, and Frémont."[2] The Civil War raised the free speech issue again, though this time critics of emancipation and the war invoked the protection of free speech. . . .

A STATE OF EMERGENCY

Lincoln faced a huge rebellion, rebel sympathizers, and resistance and spies throughout the nation. The loyalty of key states like Maryland, Missouri, and Kentucky was doubtful. The president faced one of the most extreme threats in the nation's history, and his administration responded with military arrests and suspension of the writ of habeas corpus. Lincoln explained his policy in his 1861 message to Congress:

> The whole of the laws which were required to be faithfully executed were being resisted, and failing of execution, in

2. John C. Frémont was a Republican presidential candidate.

nearly one-third of the States. Must they be allowed to finally fail of execution, even had it been perfectly clear, that by the use of the means necessary to their execution some single law, made in such tenderness of the citizens's liberty, that practically, it relieves more of the guilty, than of the innocent, should, to a very limited extent, be violated? [A]re all the laws, *but one*, to go unexecuted, and the government itself go to pieces, lest that one be violated? . . . But it was not believed that any law was violated. The provision of the Constitution that "The privilege of the writ of habeas corpus, shall not be suspended unless when, the cases of rebellion or invasion, the public safety may require it,". . . is a provision . . . that such privilege may be suspended when, in cases of rebellion, or invasion, the public safety *does* require it.

Military arrests of civilians not in the immediate theater of war and suspension of the writ of habeas corpus, however, disturbed friends as well as critics of the administration. . . . For example, Lincoln's conservative friend Orville H. Browning thought arrests ordered by the administration were "illegal and arbitrary and did more harm than good.". . .

But many others supported the administration and insisted that the Constitution provided sweeping powers to respond to the emergency. In time of civil war, they said, the Constitution justified tough measures. Supporters of the administration, and the administration itself, cited the landmark 1849 Supreme Court case of *Luther v. Borden* to justify military arrests and trials of civilians. In that case the Supreme Court had upheld the Rhode Island legislature's statewide imposition of martial law against a military and political challenge from those seeking to democratize the highly undemocratic government of the state. . . .

On March 16, 1863, Lincoln appointed General Ambrose Burnside, fresh from his unsuccessful engagement at Fredericksburg, to the post of commanding general of the Department of Ohio. On April 13, 1863, Burnside issued General Order number 38. It warned of death for those giving active physical aid to the Confederacy—such as writers and carriers of secret letters. But it went further and specifically targeted speech. "The habit of declaring sympathies for the enemy will not be allowed in this Department. Persons committing such offenses will be at once arrested. . . . [T]reason, express or implied, will not be tolerated in this Department." When the order was issued, Union armies had suffered a series of defeats in the east, antiwar sentiment was growing, and morale in the army was low.

The *Cincinnati Commercial* reported that the general was serious about Order 38 and that it covered disloyal language as well as disloyal acts: "We learn from reliable authority that General Burnside is determined to execute his Order No. 38. This order extends not only to acts in favor of rebels, but to words or expressions of sympathy in their behalf"

Many applauded the order. Colonel Joseph Geiger told a Union mass meeting that he "thanked God that in the person of General Burnside we have a man who will attend to [Northern traitors] with a strong arm . . .—who, in enforcing his General Order No. 38, will squelch out the Northern traitors here.". . .

Democrats feared that all political opposition to Lincoln administration war policy, a key political issue, was under attack. They had serious reasons for concern. For example, in Indiana, General Milo Hascall issued General Order number 9. It prohibited newspapers and public speakers from endeavoring "to bring the war policy of the Administration into disrepute," and it warned against active opposition "to the war policy of the administration.". . .

THE ARREST AND TRIAL OF VALLANDIGHAM

The arrest of Clement L. Vallandigham seemed to confirm Democrats' fear that the administration was engaged in a pervasive attack on political speech.

General Burnside knew that Vallandigham, an outspoken antiwar activist, was scheduled to speak to a May 1, 1863, Knox County Democratic political rally in Mount Vernon, Ohio.

Military agents in civilian clothes monitored the speech. Soldiers arrested Vallandigham in the early morning hours of May 5, and his trial by a military commission of seven officers began the next day, May 6. Vallandigham, an experienced trial lawyer, represented himself. The prosecution was represented by the judge advocate. By May 7 the court finished hearing evidence and argument. (This was a speedy trial indeed, and Vallandigham was unable in this very short time to subpoena one of his defense witnesses.) He was tried on the following charge: "Publicly expressing, in violation of General Orders No. 38, from Head-quarters Department of the Ohio, sympathy for those in arms against the Government of the United States, and declaring disloyal sentiments and opinions, with the object and purpose of weakening the power of the Government in its efforts to suppress an unlawful rebellion."

The charge was supported by the following specification:

In this, that the said Clement L. Vallandigham, a citizen of the State of Ohio, on or about the first day of May, 1863, at Mount Vernon, Knox County, Ohio, did publicly address a large meeting of citizens, and did utter sentiments in words, or in effect, as follows, declaring the present war "a wicked, cruel, and unnecessary war;" "a war not being waged for the preservation of the Union;" "a war for the purpose of crushing out liberty and erecting a despotism;" "a war for the freedom of the blacks and the enslavement of the whites;" stating "that if the Administration had so wished, the war could have been honorably terminated months ago;" that "peace might have been honorably obtained by listening to the proposed intermediation of France;". . . [a]ll of which opinions and sentiments he well knew did aid, comfort, and encourage those in arms against the Government, and could but induce in his hearers a distrust of their own Government, sympathy for those in arms against it, and a disposition to resist the laws of the land.

General Burnside ordered Vallandigham's arrest without consulting the president. But the general acted in a context set by the president himself. At first, Burnside seemed to have

A Plea for Free Speech

Born a slave in 1818, Frederick Douglass escaped to the North in 1838 and became a leader of the abolitionist movement, which sought to end slavery within the United States prior to the Civil War. A brilliant speaker and the publisher of the antislavery news-paper, North Star, *Douglass spoke in 1860 at Boston's Music Hall the week after an antislavery meeting had been broken up by an angry mob.*

Boston is a great city. . . . Nowhere more than here have the principles of human freedom been expounded. . . . Here, if nowhere else, we thought the right of the people to assemble and to express their opinion was secure. . . .

But here we are to-day contending for what we thought we gained years ago. The mortifying and disgraceful fact stares us in the face, that though Faneuil Hall and Bunker Hill Monument stand, freedom of speech is struck down. . . .

The world knows that last Monday a meeting assembled to discuss the question: "How Shall Slavery Be Abolished?" The world also knows that that meeting was invaded, in-sulted, captured by a mob of gentlemen, and thereafter bro-ken up and dispersed by the order of the mayor, who re-fused to protect it, though called upon to do so. . . .

No right was deemed by the fathers of the Government more sacred than the right of speech. It was in their eyes, as in the eyes of all thoughtful men, the great moral reno-vator of society and government. Daniel Webster called it a homebred right, a fireside privilege. Liberty is meaning-less where the right to utter one's thoughts and opinions has ceased to exist. That, of all rights, is the dread of tyrants. It is the right which they first of all strike down. They know its power. Thrones, dominions, principalities, and powers, founded in injustice and wrong, are sure to tremble, if men are allowed to reason of righteousness, temperance, and of a judgment to come in their presence. Slavery cannot tolerate free speech. Five years of its exercise would banish the auction block and break every chain in the South. They will have none of it there, for they have the power. But shall it be so here?

Even here in Boston, and among the friends of freedom, we hear two voices: one denouncing the mob that broke up our meeting on Monday as a base and cowardly outrage; and another, deprecating and regretting the holding of such a meeting, by such men, at such a time. We are told that the meeting was ill-timed, and the parties to it unwise.

Why, what is the matter with us? Are we going to palliate and excuse a palpable and flagrant outrage on the right of speech, by implying that only a particular description of persons should exercise that right? . . .

It would be no vindication of the right of speech to prove that certain gentlemen of great distinction, eminent for their learning and ability, are allowed to freely express their opinions on all subjects—including the subject of slavery. Such a vindication would need, itself, to be vindicated. It would add insult to injury. . . . There can be no right of speech where any man, however lifted up, or however humble, however young, or however old, is overawed by force, and compelled to suppress his honest sentiments. . . .

The principle must rest upon its own proper basis. And until the right is accorded to the humblest as freely as to the most exalted citizen, the government of Boston is but an empty name, and its freedom a mockery. A man's right to speak does not depend upon where he was born or upon his color. The simple quality of manhood is the solid basis of the right—and there let it rest forever.

Frederick Douglass, "A Plea for Free Speech in Boston," 1860.

presidential support. On May 8, 1863, having learned of the arrest from the newspapers, President Lincoln wired General Burnside: "In your determination to support the authority of the Government and suppress treason in your department, you may count on the firm support of the President."

Vallandigham sought a writ of habeas corpus from the federal court. Judge Humphrey H. Leavitt, who had been appointed to the bench by President Andrew Jackson, denied Vallandigham's petition for the writ. After conceding that if the criminal procedure guarantees of the Bill of Rights were applicable then the arrest would not be legal, Leavitt pointed to other factors including "the present state of the country, and, . . . the expediency of interfering with the exercise of the military power." He said that "The Court can not shut its eyes to the grave fact that war exists, . . . threatening the subversion and destruction of the Constitution itself. In my judgment, when the life of the republic is imperiled, he mistakes his duty and obligation as a patriot who is not willing to concede to the Constitution such a capacity of adaptation to circumstances as may be necessary to meet a great emergency, and save the nation from hopeless ruin. Self-preservation is a paramount law.". . .

At the trial, Vallandigham's May 1 speech, to what was a very large Democratic county political rally, was the basis of the charge against him. . . .

According to Captain Hill, a witness for the prosecution, Vallandigham attacked Order 38, saying that

> "he was a freeman;" that he did not ask David Tod [the Governor of Ohio], or Abraham Lincoln, or Ambrose E. Burnside for his right to speak as he had done, and was doing. That his authority for so doing was higher than General Orders No. 38—it was General Orders No. 1—the Constitution. That General Orders No. 38 was a base usurpation of arbitrary power; that he had the most supreme contempt for such power. . . . That he was resolved never to submit to an order of a military dictator, prohibiting the free discussion of either civil or military authority.

"The sooner that the people informed the minions of this usurped power that they would not submit to such restrictions upon their liberties, the better."

Captain John A. Means, another witness for the prosecution, testified Vallandigham had said that the war was an abolition war, not one waged for the preservation of the Union. Vallandigham purportedly said he would spit on Order 38 and trample it underfoot.

According to Captain Means, Vallandigham also said "he would not counsel resistance to military or civil law; that was not needed." He referred to the president as "King Lincoln" and urged his listeners to come together at the ballot box and hurl the tyrant from his throne. . . .

At the close of the evidence Vallandigham entered the following protest: he said he had been "[a]rrested without due 'process of law,' without warrant from any judicial officer" and had "been served with a 'charge and specifications,' as in a Court-martial or Military Commission.". . .

Furthermore his "alleged 'offence'" was "not known to the Constitution of the United States" or in violation of any law.

It is words spoken to the people of Ohio in an open and public political meeting, lawfully and peaceably assembled, under the Constitution and upon full notice. It is words of criticism of the public policy of the public servants of the people, by which policy it was alleged that the welfare of the country was not promoted. It was an appeal to the people to change that policy, not by force, but by free elections and the ballot-box. It is not pretended that I counseled disobedience to the Constitution, or resistance to laws and lawful authority. I never have. Beyond this protest, I have nothing further to submit.

As noted above, the United States district court refused to release Vallandigham on a writ of habeas corpus, the military tribunal convicted, and the Supreme Court declined to review the military conviction. The denial of the writ was apparently not appealed. President Lincoln changed Vallandigham's sentence from imprisonment to banishment to the Confederacy. In the Confederacy, Vallandigham boarded a blockade runner, which took him to Bermuda. From there he sailed to Canada. The Democrats of Ohio nominated him for governor, and from his remote Canadian base he proceeded to wage his campaign for governor. He was resoundingly defeated. . . .

THE FREE SPEECH TRADITION CONFRONTS THE WAR POWER

The arrest of Vallandigham was widely reported in the nation's press. Some Republican papers greeted the Vallandigham arrest as long overdue. "The arrest of this individual by order of Gen. Burnside," the *Cincinnati Commercial* noted with apparent satisfaction, "is an act that will convince the most heedless that Order No. 38 will be enforced, and the lines definitely drawn between traitors and patriots.". . .

A few days later the *Commercial* returned to its defense of Order 38. "[T]here is nothing in the celebrated Order 38 which should disturb the feelings of any loyal man. It is not designed to abridge the liberty of the individual, where that liberty is not used to the detriment of the Government." While temperate discussion would be permitted, the paper noted, violent and incendiary language and arguments that would lead to law violation would not be allowed. Most Ohio Republican papers and politicians endorsed the arrest. . . .

For many Democrats, the Vallandigham arrest was not an isolated event, but part of a larger attack on political freedom. For that reason, many Democrats who rejected Vallandigham's peace proposals rallied to his defense. Some criticisms of the arrest were general. Others focused more particularly on free speech values. Many noted that Vallandigham was not accused of violating any specific statute.

The *Albany Argus* denounced the arrest as a "crime against the Constitution," and the *Detroit Free Press* lamented that the "arrest of Mr. Vallandigham, and his hasty trial before a secret military court is an event which arouses the indignation of all lovers of the constitution and laws.". . .

The *Detroit Free Press* recited the charge against Vallandigham. The charge did not allege that Vallandigham had "violated any law of the United States," but simply an order issued by a general. "There is no pretence that he transcended the privileges guaranteed to him by the constitution and laws." Indeed, there was no proof offered that he "has even persuaded one man not to enlist, one to desert his flag, one to falter in his duty to the Union." In essence, the Vallandigham case was "an announcement that no man, in these free and loyal States, shall utter a sentiment which the hero of Fredericksburg [i.e. Burnside] disapproves of.... [I]t is monstrous to hold that men who may be taxed or drafted, shall not advocate peace whenever and wherever they please; provided they do it in accordance with the constitution and the laws."...

FREE SPEECH AND REPRESENTATIVE DEMOCRACY

George V.N. Lothrop, a scholarly leader of the bar and former Michigan attorney general, spoke to a huge protest meeting held at the Detroit City Hall. Lothrop was a Democrat who opposed Vallandigham's views and who, by his own account, had "unreservedly" supported the government "against the insurrection."

Still, Lothrop insisted on a broad and tough definition of freedom of speech. He said that soldiers had arrested Vallandigham for allegedly "expressing sympathy for rebels, declaring disloyal sentiments and opinions with a view to weaken the power of the government." Without "inquiring whether the words [Vallandigham] used will fairly bear this construction," Lothrop rejected the claim that they did or could state a legal offense. "I dwell not on the uncertainty of what is disloyal; but the point I make is whether a man can be arrested for any quality of opinions on public affairs?" Lothrop said it was a postulate that "*without free discussion there can be no free government....* Hence we can readily see at what price we must lay down this right."

For Lothrop, the right to free speech had a tough central

core, impervious to government invasion. "What is free speech under the constitution? Clearly the right to canvass and discuss without reserve public measures and acts. Anything short of this is inadequate."

Lothrop responded to a friend who claimed that freedom of speech did not protect "license."

> He meant that the expression of opinions regarded as unsound, unpatriotic, or of evil tendency, should be deemed not a true freedom, but a license to be restrained. But this obviously destroys all free discussion. . . .

The constitutional guarantee, Lothrop insisted, was framed "to protect what you call license." After all, it was "the *unpopular* opinion of to-day that needs these guaranties." The idea of limiting free speech to ideas that were popular would mean free speech principles only applied when they were not needed. "The man who runs with the majority needs no guaranty. He is never disloyal.". . .

With increasing emphasis, critics noted the threat to popular government posed by actions of the administration. Free speech was essential to democracy. "If freedom of speech is surrendered," the *Detroit Free Press* noted, "it will no longer be pretended, we presume, that the ballot-box can represent the views and wishes of the majority of the people. . . . Without freedom of speech, the ballot box is a farce." If the president had the war power to stifle speech, then he could make elections meaningless (for elections without free speech were a mockery). By the same war power logic, the president could simply dispense with elections. . . .

THE DEFENSE OF THE ADMINISTRATION

Defenders of the administration took several tacks. First, they said it was graceless for a party, many of whose members had supported suppression of antislavery speech, to criticize this suppression of free speech. "Since the arrest of the treason-shrieker, Vallandigham," the *Chicago Tribune* noted, "his disciples fill the air with cries about the Constitutional right of 'free speech.' [W]e wish to ask those Copperhead defenders of free speech how much of this *Constitutional and sacred privilege* did their party allow to be exercised in the South before the war broke out?"

The paper asked, "How much 'free speech' was tolerated in Secession during the twenty years before the war broke out?" Opponents of slavery were "arrested, imprisoned, fined, tar and feathered, rode on a rail, whipped, ducked, and even hung for daring to exercise [their] 'Constitutional right of free speech.'"...

The Special Circumstances of War

Those who supported suppressing Vallandigham... insisted that free speech did not protect license. Politicians and citizens, General Burnside had announced, "must not use license and plead that they are exercising liberty." After all, the nation was at war. In times of peace, a writer in the *Chicago Tribune* announced, free speech could be tolerated as a "harmless right." But things were quite different "in times of war and revolution." Ordinarily, "even the licentiousness of speech is better than a too rigid restriction of it; but we can't afford to be quite so generous," the writer noted, "at the present time, when ... the very existence of the nation" is at stake.

"The advocates of treason," Republican congressman Jehu Baker of Illinois said, "talk of liberty of speech and the press, without once thinking of the distinction between the liberty of a man and the license of a beast."...

President Lincoln crafted two politically potent defenses of his policy. The first came in response to a letter from a New York group critical of the Vallandigham arrest; the second responded to the Ohio Democrats' demand for Vallandigham's release....

President Lincoln made telling use of the necessity argument in reply to his critics....

Lincoln rejected the claim that Vallandigham, as a person who was not in the military and not in a theater of war, was entitled to the criminal procedure guarantees of the Bill of

Rights. Lincoln noted that the Civil War was a case of rebellion and that in such a case the Constitution authorized the suspension of the writ of habeas corpus when public safety required it. Arrests by ordinary civil process and those required in cases of rebellion were different. In the case of rebellion, "arrests are made, not so much for what has been done, as for what probably would be done. The latter is more for the preventative and less for the vindictive than the former." So, in rebellions, basic Bill of Rights guarantees did not apply because it was necessary to restrain people who were guilty of no civil crime. "The man who stands by and says nothing when the peril of his Government is discussed, cannot be misunderstood," Lincoln announced. "If not hindered, he is sure to help the enemy; much more, if he talks ambiguously—talks for his country with 'buts' and 'ifs' and 'ands.'"

The New Yorkers had insisted that no military arrests should be made "outside of the lines of necessary military occupation, and the scenes of insurrection." Lincoln rejected the distinction: "Inasmuch, however, as the Constitution itself makes no such distinction, I am unable to believe that there *is* any such constitutional distinction."

Lincoln denied that Vallandigham was arrested for criticism of administration policy and of the edict of General Burnside.

> It is asserted, in substance, that Mr. Vallandigham was, by a military commander, seized and tried "for no other reason than words addressed to a public meeting, in criticism of the course of the Administration, and in condemnation of the Military orders of the General." Now, if there be no mistake about this; if this assertion is the truth and the whole truth; if there was no other reason for the arrest, then I concede that the arrest was wrong. But the arrest, as I understand, was made for a very different reason. Mr. Vallandigham avows his hostility to the War on the part of the Union; and his arrest was made because he was laboring, with some effect, to prevent the raising of troops; to encourage desertions from the army; and to leave the Rebellion without an adequate military force to suppress it.

In his later reply to the Ohio Democrats who demanded Vallandigham's return, Lincoln admitted, "I certainly do not know that Mr. V. has specifically, and by direct language, advised against enlistments, and in favor of desertion, and resistance to drafting." But that was the effect of his words: "[T]his hindrance of the military, including maiming and murder, is due to the course in which Mr. V. has been engaged" more than to any other cause, Lincoln said, and to Vallandigham personally more than to any other man.

In his response to the New Yorkers, Lincoln asserted that the rebellion could only be suppressed by military force. Military force required armies. "Long experience has shown," Lincoln noted, "that armies cannot be maintained unless desertions shall be punished by the severe penalty of death. . . . Must I shoot a simple-minded soldier boy who deserts, while I must not touch a hair of a wily agitator who induces him to desert?". . .

Finally, Lincoln denied that his acts would prove to be a precedent for repression in time of peace: "I can no more be persuaded that the Government can constitutionally take no strong measures in time of rebellion, because it can be shown that the same could not be lawfully taken in time of peace, than I can be persuaded that a particular drug is not good medicine for a sick man, because it can be shown not to be good food for a well one."

EVALUATING THE SUPPRESSION

The Vallandigham [case] pitted free speech against the power of the president as commander in chief. The most powerful argument for free speech during wartime came from the nature of the American government—from democracy. This free speech argument insisted that democracy entailed the right of the people who would be affected by government policy to attempt to persuade other citizens to change it. Because the right was a continuing one, government policy had to be open to criticism and revision. . . . Free speech could not legitimately be foreclosed by government policy because that foreclosure would rob the people of their collective right to determine their fate and their individual right to try to persuade others to change course. By this understanding, individuals would retain a personal right to speak even if the majority had decided it had heard enough and wanted to shut them up. Though popular sovereignty is a metaphor (and therefore highlights one aspect of the truth while hiding others), the aspect it highlights is powerful and important.

In setting out these principles, critics of suppression of speech were essentially correct. In representative government people have a right to seek to control their fate both by deciding who should represent them and by keeping their representatives informed of their needs and desires. People liable to be conscripted, shot, maimed, or killed (and to have these things happen to friends and loved ones) should have a continuing right to consider the wisdom of the war in which such sacrifices are demanded. The alternative is to turn the lives of the many over to the unchecked and unscrutinized power of a few. Free speech is essential to preserving the structure of representative government under the Constitution and also reflects a basic right of individuals to talk about crucial issues that shape their lives. . . .

Lincoln himself recognized the tension between the war power and democracy, and this recognition plus strong public opposition to suppression of speech helped keep suppression from becoming more pervasive. Lincoln was convinced that in cases of rebellion strong but temporary measures were permitted to save democracy. He could no more believe that military arrests in time of rebellion would lead to the loss of "Public Discussion, the Liberty of Speech and the Press" in the peaceful future than he could "believe that a man could contract so strong an appetite for emetics during temporary illness as to persist in feeding upon them during the remainder of his healthful life.". . .

In any case, Lincoln was unwilling to carry his rebellion-war power logic to its ultimate conclusion—which would have justified suspension of elections. In October 1864, Lincoln responded to those who had suggested that, even if the

Democrats should win, he would not accept electoral defeat. "I am struggling," Lincoln said, "to maintain the government, not to overthrow it."...

On November 10, 1864, Lincoln elaborated his conclusion. An election in the midst of a great civil war was dangerous, because it divided a nation that needed all its strength to put down the rebellion. But, in spite of the danger, "the election was a necessity." He added, "We can not have free government without elections; and if the rebellion could force us to forego, or postpone a national election, it might fairly claim to have already conquered and ruined us." It is equally true that we cannot have free elections without free speech....

Lincoln failed to come to grips with the extent to which arrests like those of Vallandigham threatened the value of popular rule that he cherished. Basically, he accepted the idea that the bad tendency of speeches like Vallandigham's and the importance of other constitutional values justified suppression....

Acceptance and full implementation of Lincoln's principle outlaws antiwar political speech and puts the democratic process in abeyance for the duration of the war. That is so because a strong criticism of war *will*, as advocates of suppression insist, increase the number of those who are unwilling to risk their lives for the cause. But silencing the antiwar politician, rather than disciplining the deserter, ends democracy in wartime. That, plus the strong negative reaction it produced, may be why such suppression never became more pervasive.

The American Civil Liberties Union Fights for Free Speech

A graduate of the University of Michigan, Samuel Walker received his master's degree from the University of Nebraska at Omaha in 1970 and his PhD from Ohio State University three years later. He currently serves as the Isaacson Professor of Criminal Justice at the University of Nebraska at Omaha. He is the author of eleven books and dozens of articles on police practices, criminal justice, hate speech, and civil liberties. He is also a longtime member of the American Civil Liberties Union (ACLU), an organization dedicated to defending the Bill of Rights, serving on the organization's board of directors since 1983. In 1991 he was named "Civil Libertarian of the Year" by the Nebraska Civil Liberties Union.

In this excerpt from his 1990 book *In Defense of American Liberties: A History of the ACLU*, Walker describes how the American Civil Liberties Union embraced the cause of free speech and began to win important legal battles against censorship. Founded in 1920 by Roger Baldwin in the aftermath of government crackdowns on World War I dissenters, the ACLU initially defended the right of war protesters and other dissidents to criticize the government. Gradually the organization broadened its focus to defend not only political speech, but all expression.

Two events in 1925 signaled a shift in national attitudes toward civil liberties. The sensational Scopes "monkey trial"

Samuel Walker, *In Defense of American Liberties: A History of the ACLU.* New York: Oxford University Press, 1990. Copyright © 1990 by Samuel Walker. All rights reserved. Reproduced by permission of the publisher.

140 • THE FREE SPEECH MOVEMENT

thrust the ACLU into the national spotlight as the defender of the freedom to learn. Then, in *Gitlow v. New York* the Supreme Court accepted the principle that the Fourteenth Amendment incorporated the protections of the Bill of Rights. By the mid-1920s, new social and political forces were encouraging respect for civil liberties principles.

SCOPES: THE GREAT "MONKEY TRIAL"

While routinely clipping the newspapers for civil liberties news in the spring of 1925, ACLU secretary Lucille Milner noticed an intriguing item. Tennessee had just passed a law forbidding the teaching of evolution. She brought the clipping to Roger Baldwin and said, "Here's something that ought to have our attention." Baldwin agreed and, in a newspaper article, offered ACLU assistance to anyone willing to challenge the law. This set in motion one of the most famous courtroom battles in American history. The Scopes "monkey trial" became a fight over the freedom to learn and specifically the freedom from state-imposed religious dogma. The ACLU rarely provided counsel at the trial level, and so Baldwin's offer reflected his growing concern over political restraints on teachers. Indeed, he had recently created the ACLU Academic Freedom Committee.

The Tennessee law prohibited teachers in state-supported schools and universities from teaching "any theory that denies the story of the Divine Creation of man as taught in the Bible." It was symptomatic of a wave of Protestant fundamentalism sweeping the country. This movement was a rearguard action, protesting the advance of science, secularism, cultural pluralism, and changing sexual mores. Although the public schools had always been permeated with Protestant dogma, it had never been imposed by state law. Nor had any state ever prohibited the teaching of a new scientific idea. The real significance of the Scopes case lay in the fact that the forces of science and secular education were strong enough to oppose the fundamentalists. *Scopes* introduced a new chapter in American politics, a long-running struggle over the place of religion in American life in general and in the public schools in particular.

Dayton, Tennessee, businessman George Rappelyea, whose interest lay less in academic freedom than in boosting the local economy, instigated the case as a scheme to promote Dayton, by persuading a young science teacher, John Thomas Scopes, to violate the law. Angling for publicity, they sent a telegram to William Jennings Bryan, asking him to enter the case. The three-time Democratic presidential candidate was the most widely known fundamentalist in the country. Bryan, already in Tennessee to address the national convention of the World Christian Fundamentals Association, accepted, and Clarence Darrow offered to represent Scopes. The flamboyant sixty-eight-year-old lawyer was at least as famous as Bryan was, notorious as a self-proclaimed atheist, opponent of capital punishment, and defender of unpopular cases. Only a year before, the famous "attorney for the damned" had saved the young murderers Nathan Leopold and Richard Loeb from the death penalty in a sensational trial. Scopes accepted Darrow's offer, and the case suddenly became a confrontation over the literal interpretation of the Bible.

The case was a publicity bonanza for the ACLU. "Our office was filled with all the top journalists," Baldwin recalled. Never before had the ACLU received such favorable attention. For the first time it defended a cause with which the national press and its readers could identify. That is, they had little interest in the rights of Communists but saw science and education as the key to progress. . . .

The trial immediately went badly for Darrow, whom the prosecution outwitted, by persuading Judge John Raulston to confine the case to the narrow question of the right of the legislature to control public school curricula and to exclude all the expert testimony about science and religion that the ACLU had patiently assembled from noted scientists and theologians. The former were prepared to testify that the Tennessee law was unreasonable in light of modern science, whereas the latter would argue that even sincere Christians disagreed over the meaning of the Genesis story. At a stroke, therefore, Judge Raulston virtually destroyed the ACLU's entire case.

With his case in shambles, Darrow spent the weekend devising a scheme to get the evolution issue into court by trapping Bryan himself into testifying. Bryan could not resist the opportunity to proclaim his religious faith from the witness stand and fell headlong into the snare. Under Darrow's mercilous questioning, he made a fool of himself. For instance, Darrow got him to say, "I do not think about things I don't think about" and, in a crucial exchange over Genesis, admitted that he did not believe the earth was created in "six days of twenty-four hours." Audible gasps could be heard in the courtroom as Bryan undermined his own case for a literal interpretation of the Bible. He sputtered on desperately, dimly aware that something had gone wrong. Mercifully, Judge Raulston adjourned the trial, and the next day a clearly embarrassed prosecutor ended the trial. The jury took just nine minutes to find John T. Scopes guilty. Judge Raulston then made a serious mistake by incorrectly instructing the jury: Under Tennessee law fines over $50 had to be set by the jury, but the misinstructed jury allowed Raulston himself to impose a $100 fine.

A devastated Bryan died a week after the trial. In New York, ACLU leaders were appalled by Darrow's conduct and sought to remove him from the appeal. [Cocounsel Arthur Garfields] Hays again defended his partner. "The Strategy of the Scopes Defense" was to raise the political question of "whether among civilized people ignorance and intolerance, even when indulged in by the majority and made into law, should be permitted to stifle education." The trial was a platform for raising broad issues of human freedom. Darrow and Hays forged a warm friendship and went on to collaborate on other celebrated cases. Immediately after the trial they went to Detroit where they defended the black doctor Ossian Sweet, charged with murder, in one of the most famous civil rights cases of the 1920s. A year later they challenged censorship in Boston by personally selling a banned magazine on Boston Common.

In 1927 the Tennessee Supreme Court reversed Scopes's conviction because of Judge Raulston's error. Expressing its embarrassment over the entire affair, the court said it saw "nothing to be gained by prolonging the life of this bizarre case.". . .

VICTORY IN PATERSON

Hard on the heels of Scopes, the ACLU won its first free speech victory in court—appropriately in a case involving Roger Baldwin. The case began in 1924 when eight thousand silk workers went out on strike in Paterson, New Jersey. The mill owners obtained an injunction banning picketing and forbidding strikers from congregating in crowds. By October, fifteen separate injunctions had shut down virtually all union activity. The silk workers then turned to the ACLU for help. Baldwin organized a free speech demonstration and led to City Hall thirty protestors carrying American flags. Union leader John C. Butterworth began to read the First Amendment, but police arrested him before he could finish. Baldwin turned himself in the next day, explaining his role in organizing the demonstration. The publicity had the desired effect, and the police permitted several rallies over the next few weeks.

Baldwin was subsequently convicted under a 1796 unlawful assembly law. His appeal touched off a bitter fight among ACLU lawyers which brought to the surface the underlying differences over legal strategy. Hays and Samuel Untermyer (who had advised the prosecution in the Scopes case) drafted a political brief discussing Anglo-American traditions of free speech. Felix Frankfurter objected strenuously: "I have no sympathy at all with the aim of counsel who shape their briefs with a view to securing a 'landmark' opinion rather than securing a favorable decision." He advised arguing the case on the narrow factual question of whether Baldwin's behavior fell within the scope of the law's prohibition of "assaults, batteries, false imprisonment, affrays, riots, unlawful assemblies, nuisances, cheats, [and] deceits" and whether any of the demonstrators were armed as charged. Hays, fresh from the theatrical Scopes trial, replied that it was important to make the court "see that there is more involved in this case than the facts of this meeting." Frankfurter told Baldwin he didn't have "much confidence" in the lawyers who seemed to be "indulging in the dramatic love of a fight."

Baldwin remained supremely indifferent to his fate. He didn't think the brief would make any difference in either event. Although conceding that Frankfurter had made some valid points, he pointed out that "my own inclinations are usually in the direction of Hays' line of tactics" and endorsed his brief. Frankfurter's "careful, lawyer-like work" was "just what the courts should never hear." He told [colleague Morris] Ernst he didn't want "a reversal on narrow or technical grounds. I want it squarely on the issue of what is unlawful assembly, and I'd like to couple with it a denunciation by the court of police lawlessness." He soon left for a year's sabbatical in Europe and was out of the country when the intermediate court of appeals sustained his conviction.

The appeal to the state's high court intensified the dispute among the lawyers. Acting ACLU Director Forrest Bailey eased out Hays and Untermyer on the pretext that New Jersey judges did not like to be "lectured" by New York lawyers. He replaced them with Arthur T. Vanderbilt, one of the most distinguished lawyers in New Jersey and the future chief justice of its supreme court. Baldwin, returning from Europe in time for the final arguments, told a New Jersey audience that "my homecoming would have lost some of the zest of American life if it had been not to keep a date with a prosecutor and judge and to hear again the familiar voice of law and order." Privately, he told Vanderbilt he was "not over-sanguine about the approaching decision" and inquired about arranging a sentence to the state prison instead of the Passaic County Jail. An equally pessimistic Vanderbilt replied that "it is a distinct relief to have a client who ... does not expect his lawyers to perform miracles."

To everyone's astonishment, the New Jersey Court of Errors and Appeals unanimously reversed Baldwin's conviction in a decision that was a ringing affirmation of freedom of speech and assembly. The decision held that the guarantees of both the New Jersey and the U.S. Constitutions, "being in favor of liberty of the people, must be given the most liberal and comprehensive construction." The purpose of Baldwin's rally "was per se not an unlawful one," and there was no proof that it constituted a threat to public order. Citing the Magna Carta, the Petition of Right, and other ancient documents, the Court's opinion was filled with the very historical and philosophical arguments Frankfurter had tried to eliminate. Baldwin, who had always dismissed the courts as effective protectors of civil liberties, won the most sweeping First Amendment victory of the entire decade. The decision was yet another sign that the tide of public and judicial opinion was slowly beginning to turn in favor of civil liberties.

BREAKTHROUGH IN THE SUPREME COURT

Just as the ACLU was preparing for the Scopes trial, it scored its first significant breakthrough in the Supreme Court. The decision in *Gitlow v. United States* offered the hope of judicial protection of civil liberties in the future.

The case involved Benjamin Gitlow, a founder of the Communist party, who had been convicted under the 1902 New York Criminal Anarchy law. At issue in his appeal was the question of whether his pamphlet, *The Left-Wing Manifesto*, was constitutionally protected speech. The revolutionary *Manifesto* declared, "The old order is in decay. Civilization is in collapse. The proletarian revolution and the communist reconstruction of society—*the struggle for these*—is now indispensable." That is, though it advocated revolution, in the abstract, it did not urge any immediate illegal action.

Walter Pollak, a New York attorney with a corporate law practice, handled the appeal for the ACLU.... "The case," Pollak argued, "brings to this Court for the first time the question of the constitutionality of making advocacy per se, and without regard to consequences, a crime." Exploring the scope of the First Amendment, Pollak distinguished between *public* and *private* speech. In private matters a person could be punished for libel, obscenity, or fraudulent promises. In the public realm, however, "the citizen's liberty to take part in public affairs stands on another and broader footing." Following Oliver Wendell Holmes's *Abrams* dissent, Pollak contended that the right of free speech was "in the interest of the whole community. The citizen has a right to express, for the State may have an interest in hearing, any doctrine" no matter how foolish or unpopular. Because Gitlow was prosecuted under state law, Pollak argued that he was protected by the First Amendment because the due process clause of the Fourteenth Amendment incorporated its guarantees. The Court had never accepted the incorporation idea.

The Court affirmed Gitlow's conviction and upheld the constitutionality of the New York Criminal Anarchy Act. But in a crucial passage, conservative Justice Edward T. Sanford held that "for the present purposes we may and do assume that freedom of speech and of the press—which are protected by the First Amendment from abridgment by Congress—are among the fundamental personal rights and 'liberties' protected by the due process clause of the Fourteenth Amendment from impairment by the states." Although cold comfort to Gitlow, this dictum was a major breakthrough, holding out the promise of future judicial protection of civil liberties.

Several legal scholars grasped the implications of this dictum. Charles Warren, a conservative professor at the Harvard Law School, saw that the Court had created a "new 'liberty,'" with enormous potential for protecting the rights enunciated in the Bill of Rights. His colleague Zechariah Chafee, Jr., called it a "victory out of defeat." But ACLU leaders were divided over the decision. Baldwin, as skeptical of the courts as ever, saw it as a crushing defeat. In the ACLU *Annual Report* he concluded that "the repressive measures passed during and since the war were strengthened by the U.S. Supreme Court in the *Gitlow* case." Pollak and [assistant counsel Walter] Nelles, on the other hand, saw it as a near miss and turned with renewed enthusiasm to the Charlotte Whitney appeal which loomed as the Court's next important First Amendment case.

Charlotte Anita Whitney's political odyssey resembled Baldwin's. She came from old New England stock, had graduated from Wellesley, and had become a Progressive reformer. She had been radicalized by the war and so had joined the Communist Labor party. Her conviction struck even more deeply at freedom of political association, as she had been convicted for simply organizing a political party: She had neither given an incendiary speech nor distributed any revolutionary pamphlet. In 1927 the Court dashed the hopes raised by *Gitlow* and unanimously sustained her conviction. It held that California had a legitimate right to "punish those who abuse" freedom of speech "by utterances inimical to the public welfare, tending to incite to crime, disturb the public peace, or endanger the foundations of organized government and threaten its overthrow by unlawful means."

Despite the defeat, Justice Louis Brandeis wrote a concurring opinion that became one of the most eloquent statements on freedom of speech. "Those who won our independence by revolution," Brandeis observed, "were not cowards. They did not fear political change. They did not exalt order at the cost of liberty." Revising Justice Oliver Wendell Holmes's "clear and present danger" test, he held that "no danger flowing from speech can be deemed clear and present, unless the incidence of the evil apprehended is so imminent that it may befall before there is opportunity for full discussion." Proximity and danger were the crucial elements. If there were time to discuss the ideas involved, no matter how false or foolish, "the remedy to be applied is more speech, not enforced silence."

A second 1927 case, little noted then and forgotten today, was actually the first free speech victory in the Supreme Court. IWW (Industrial Workers of the World) organizer Harold Fiske had been convicted under the Kansas Criminal Syndicalism law, but the only evidence against him was his possession of the preamble to the IWW's constitution. Thus, with the ACLU financing the appeal, the Court overturned his conviction on the grounds of insufficient evidence. Because the IWW's preamble did not mention violence, no inference could be made that his activities fell within the scope of the Kansas law. The decision did not touch on the constitutionality of the law and contained no eloquent opinions, but Harold Fiske was the first person to have his First Amendment rights upheld by the Supreme Court. As Chafee observed, "In *Fiske*, the Supreme Court for the first time made freedom of speech mean something.". . .

New Horizons in Freedom of Expression

With thousands of people milling around the Boston Common on April 5, 1926, Arthur Garfield Hays and H.L. Mencken sold copies of Mencken's *American Mercury*, banned that month by the Boston Watch and Ward Society because Herbert Asbury's article, "Hatrack," made fun of fundamentalists. Hays and Mencken went to Boston, obtained a peddler's license, and provoked an arrest. Hays won an acquittal for Mencken and a court order restraining the Watch and Ward Society. The society, an odd coalition of Protestant Brahmins and puritanical Catholics, retaliated with an even more energetic crusade against indecency. The ensuing "Boston Massacre" popularized the phrase "Banned in Boston" and launched the ACLU's first serious attack on censorship in the arts.

The sixty-five books banned in Boston included Theodore Dreiser's *An American Tragedy*, Sinclair Lewis's *Elmer Gantry*, Ernest Hemingway's *The Sun Also Rises*, and John Dos Passos's *Manhattan Transfer*. Boston readers were also denied books by Bertrand Russell, William Faulkner, Upton Sinclair, Babette Deutsch, and Olive Schreiner and productions of Eugene O'Neill's *Desire Under the Elms* and *Strange Interlude*. The official city censor, John Michael Casey, explained that his test was "whether he would want his mother, wife, daughter or sister to see such a play." He banned *Strange Interlude* because it mentioned abortion. Most booksellers and theater owners voluntarily withdrew works in the face of veiled threats.

Until the Boston crisis, the ACLU had taken little interest in censorship of the arts. Following the dominant school of First Amendment theory articulated by Zechariah Chafee (and later Alexander Meikeljohn), it had focused on political speech. Other forms of expression were not central to the process of self-government and so did not deserve the same protection. Baldwin and his closest ACLU friends, Norman Thomas and John Haynes Holmes, were extremely puritanical: Holmes thought local communities could restrict "indecent" material and expressed shock at "all those four-letter words" in *Lady Chatterly's Lover.* In 1931 Thomas approved a ban on *Birth of a Nation* because it might stir up mob violence. In March 1927, the ACLU's acting director, Forrest Bailey, told a Massachusetts librarian that "I hope you will not be too greatly disappointed when I tell you we cannot go into the 'anti-obscenity' campaign in Boston. That is a phase of free speech which we have kept clear of . . . to avoid complicating our main issues."

Consequently, Hays and Ernst led the fight for a broader ACLU attack on censorship. Thoroughly secularized Jews, they shared none of the puritanism of the ACLU Protestants. They were not embarrassed by sex and believed that personal freedom extended into the realm of private sexual relations. Hays even proposed an early version of no-fault divorce and was the first ACLU leader to articulate a rudimentary "absolutist" position of no restrictions on "the expression of opinion of any kind, at any time, by anyone or anywhere." . . .

The ACLU pamphlet *Censorship in Boston* (signed by Chafee but actually written by Baldwin) was a benchmark in its evolving view of the First Amendment. While opposing all prior restraints, it approved subsequent criminal proceedings against indecent books and plays. The ACLU, operating on the assumption that ordinary citizens were more tolerant than government bureaucrats were, sought at this point to transfer the power to determine what was indecent from public officials to juries. The juries, however, should "take into consideration the entire book at issue and not isloated parts." The ACLU was not yet ready to defend "indecency," much less obscenity.

Also, the pamphlet made a significant concession on political speech: "If a speaker in a Boston public hall utters indecencies, or advocates crimes such as the overthrow of the government by violence, he can be punished after conviction by a jury." Not as broad a protection of political speech as the ACLU had argued elsewhere, *Censorship in Boston* may have been tailored to avoid offending potential allies.

But the ACLU's efforts did not end censorship in Boston, for *Strange Interlude, An American Tragedy*, and birth control meetings were still banned in the 1930s. The campaign, however, had a profound effect on the ACLU. Coming hard on the heels of the Scopes case, it reinforced the growing sense that the public was ready for a broader anticensorship campaign. . . .

MARY WARE DENNETT AND *THE SEX SIDE OF LIFE*

Mary Ware Dennett's pamphlet *The Sex Side of Life* finally forced the ACLU to come to terms with sex. A long-time ACLU activist, Dennett had been secretary of the National American Women's Suffrage Association and had worked closely with Baldwin during World War I. Although forgotten in later years, in the 1920s she was Margaret Sanger's chief rival as the leader of the birth control movement. Unable in 1915 to find any adequate sex education materials for her children, she wrote her own. Friends began borrowing copies, and soon *The Sex Side of Life* had a large audience. The *Medical Review of Reviews* published it in 1918, and a reprint eventually, sold over 35,000 copies through only one small advertisement.

Dennett's short pamphlet contained an elementary description of male and female anatomy and a discussion of sexual intercourse, masturbation, and sexually transmitted diseases, concluding with a moralistic tribute to married love. The U.S. Postal Service declared it obscene in 1922 but never tried to stop its circulation. In 1928 Dennett was entrapped by a member of the Daughters of the American Revolution who requested a copy under a fictitious name. But the prosecution backfired as influential members of the medical community and conservative Republican clubwomen rose to Dennett's defense. The response was a revealing index of changing public mores. In just twenty years birth control had moved from being a radical idea—the property of Emma Goldman and Elizabeth Gurley Flynn—to an eminently respectable cause in wealthy and conservative circles.

Ernst represented Dennett at trial, and the ACLU coordinated publicity and fund-raising. The jury took only forty minutes to convict her, agreeing with the government that the pamphlet was "pure and simple smut." The judge fined her $300. The ACLU reported that the conviction "aroused wider interest than [had] any censorship case in years." Publisher Roy Howard and Mrs. Marshall Field of Chicago lent their names to the defense committee, along with John Dewey and many eminent doctors and social workers. Dewey found it "almost incredible" that anyone should object to this fine pamphlet. Ernst won reversal of the conviction on appeal. Augustus Hand, cousin of Learned Hand, ruled that Dennett's pamphlet did not fall within the scope of the Comstock law's ban on "obscene, lewd or lascivious" material. Rather, it should be judged in terms of its "main effect," which, in this case, was to "promote understanding and self-control." Hand also remarked that adolescents should not be left without any alternative but "the casual gossip of ignorant playmates."

Even before the case was over, the Dennett Defense Committee called for a "permanent agency" to fight restrictions on birth control information, turning over to the ACLU its $1,265 surplus. Baldwin thereupon organized the Committee Against Stage Censorship in early 1931, with Ernst, Harry Elmer Barnes, Walter Lippmann, H.L. Mencken, Eugene O'Neill, Lewis Mumford, and Elmer Rice as members. All agreed that the problem was much broader than just the theater and proposed a national effort to fight censorship in the "literary arts, the press, motion and talking pictures, the radio, and the scientific discussion of sex." The new National Committee on Freedom from Censorship (NCFC) marked the beginning of the ACLU's frontal assault on all forms of censorship.

The Dennett case was an indication of changing public attitudes toward sexuality and the coming revolution in sex roles. Birth control pioneers Emma Goldman, Margaret Sanger, and Dennett understood that control of reproduction was one of the keys to changing the power and status of women in society generally. This, in turn, required readily available information. Hays and Ernst were the first in the ACLU to understand the link between censorship and sex roles.

A year after the Dennett decision, Ernst successfully challenged a U.S. Customs Service ban on Marie Stopes's *Married Love*, a discussion of female sexuality. Three months later he won another victory, defeating the U.S. Customs Service's ban on Stopes's *Contraception*. With characteristic hyperbole, Ernst proclaimed: "Sex wins in America." Judge John M. Woolsey's opinion, however, applied only to literature imported by a doctor and said nothing about contraceptive devices.

Finally, in 1933 Ernst won one of American history's greatest victories over censorship. On behalf of the Random House publishing firm, he defeated the Customs ban on James Joyce's *Ulysses*. Taking into account the work as a whole, Judge Woolsey held that *Ulysses* was not obscene. The defeat was such an embarrassment to the Customs Service that it promptly hired Huntington Cairns as a special advisory on obscenity matters and greatly reduced the number of books it banned. By the early 1930s, the tide was running against censorship. . . .

VINDICATION

In 1931 the Supreme Court vindicated the ACLU's efforts with two landmark decisions affirming First Amendment protection of freedom of speech and press. The first involved Communist party member Yetta Stromberg, convicted under the California law outlawing display of "a red flag, banner or badge . . . as a sign, symbol or emblem of opposition to organized government." Stromberg was a counselor at a Communist summer camp for children. Although the children saluted the Soviet flag every morning, Stromberg was not charged with inciting revolutionary violence. The ACLU, sharing the appeal to the Supreme Court with the International Labor Defense, was optimistic about the case. As attorney John Beardsley said, "We have a fighting chance."

The Court justified this optimism, overturning Stromberg's conviction and invalidating the red flag section of the California law. Chief Justice Charles Evans Hughes's opinion affirmed a broad principle of freedom of association: "The maintenance of the opportunity for free political discussion . . . is a fundamental principle of our constitutional system." The ban on red flags was "vague and indefinite" and "repugnant to the guaranty of liberty contained in the Fourteenth Amendment." *Stromberg* was a dramatic break from the entire line of Court decisions reaching back to the 1919 *Schenck* case. It affirmed the ideas expressed in Holmes's *Abrams* dissent and vindicated ACLU's eleven-year fight for free speech.

Stromberg was no fluke, as the Court immediately followed it with another ground-breaking First Amendment decision. *Near v. Minnesota* affirmed the principle that the First Amendment protected the press against prior restraint. As was true of so many landmark cases, this basic freedom was won by a thoroughly disreputable plaintiff. In his scurrilous weekly, *The Saturday Press*, Jay Near indulged his anti-Catholic, anti-Semitic, antiblack, and antilabor prejudices in a long scandal-mongering career in Minneapolis. In the episode that provoked his Court case, he leveled sweeping charges of corruption and nonfeasance against the mayor, the police chief, the county attorney, and the major daily newspapers in Minneapolis. The authorities closed down *The Saturday Press* under a 1925 public nuisance abatement law. The ACLU offered to defend Near but, to its chagrin, was maneuvered out of the case by Colonel Robert McCormick, publisher of the *Chicago Tribune*. Having recently faced a costly libel suit by Henry Ford, the conservative McCormick had developed an interest in freedom of the press.

On June 1, 1931, the Supreme Court ruled the Minnesota law to be unconstitutional, in a decision that firmly established the freedom of the press against prior restraint, with Chief

Justice Hughes holding that "it is no longer open to doubt that the liberty of the press and of speech is within the liberties safeguarded by the due process clause of the Fourteenth Amendment from invasion by state action." The incorporation of the freedom of the press clause fulfilled the promise of *Gitlow* six years before and vindicated Walter Pollak's groundbreaking arguments on the Fourteenth Amendment.

Stromberg and *Near* marked a historic turn for the Supreme Court on the First Amendment and, in a broader sense, indicated a deeper change in public attitudes. Historian Paul Murphy noted "the singular lack of broad-scale criticism." That is, the public was apparently not alarmed at the Court's protection of Communists and publishers of scandal sheets. Broad changes in public attitudes are difficult to measure, but it appears that by the early 1930s, support for freedom of expression had gained ground. The Scopes case, the birth control movement, and the new currents in American literature had helped bring about a new spirit of tolerance for unpopular ideas. . . .

By 1932 the ACLU was out of the wilderness. After twelve years of lonely effort, civil liberties principles had established a small but significant beachhead. Perhaps even more important than the Supreme Court decisions was the change in public attitudes: Freedom of speech was no longer a heretical idea, and key opinion makers had begun to speak out on behalf of tolerance for the new and the unpopular. The country had changed in the years since World War I, and the ACLU could claim much of the credit for the new attitudes toward the Bill of Rights.

The Berkeley Free Speech Movement

DAVID BURNER

As the civil rights movement swept through the American South in the early 1960s, many students on college campuses became politically active. Many southern students, and a few from the North, took part in demonstrations against racial segregation throughout the South. Others questioned the participation of their colleges in research for national defense programs that resulted in the building of nuclear weapons and other instruments of war. As U.S. military advisers began to confront Communist ground forces in Vietnam, some students began to question the wisdom of the Cold War policies. In the midst of these controversies, students at the University of California at Berkeley placed tables along a walkway on campus and handed out literature on a variety of controversial topics (such as Vietnam and race relations) to passing students. Determining that literature promoting off-campus events and causes violated school policy, UC Berkeley college administrators banned the leafleting activity. The students reacted to this decree with a series of protests that became known as the Berkeley Free Speech Movement.

In this essay, excerpted from his book *Making Peace with the Sixties*, David Burner explores the roots and philosophy of the Free Speech Movement. He describes how the weeks of protest at Berkeley led to a relaxation of regulations on speech, changing campus life not only at Berkeley but across the nation. A political historian at the State University of New York, Stony Brook, Burner received his PhD from Columbia University in 1965. He is the author of more than a dozen books and the editor of several more.

David Burner, *Making Peace with the Sixties*. Princeton, NJ: Princeton University Press, 1996. Copyright © 1996 by Princeton University Press. Reproduced by permission of Princeton University Press.

B etween 1963 and 1964 the number of entering freshman at the University of California at Berkeley increased by 37 percent. In the previous decade students majoring in the more socially conscious humanities and social sciences had jumped from 36 to 50 percent. Clark Kerr, president of the multicampus University of California system, had planned for the arrival of masses of new students. But he failed to see the attendant problems. He presided over an institution, committed to acting *in loco parentis* [in place of parents], that in this new time of student ferment and enormous growth could no longer do so. Academic conservatives complained that administrators and faculty members were no longer supervising their young charges' thought and behavior; students were soon complaining of the vestiges of that supervision.

Kerr, a liberal Quaker and a Democrat, had helped squelch a faculty loyalty oath imposed by the California legislature back in the McCarthy era. Yet he often compromised. In 1961, he refused to allow Malcolm X to appear on campus; his grounds were that Malcolm was a sectarian religious leader. But he did not block the less controversial Billy Graham, the prominent evangelical preacher. On another occasion he kept Herbert Aptheker, editor of the American Communist party's theoretical journal, from speaking. In 1963 Kerr lifted a ban against communist speakers, but to get the university Regents' approval he instituted a yardstick he himself disliked: spokesmen for traditional views would have to follow controversial speakers. In all, he was a prototype of the liberal who would be caught in the conflicting demands of his time. That is likely a fair description of much of the administration at Berkeley. The maneuvers, at times ham-handed and at others conciliatory, of Berkeley officialdom in 1964 and 1965 attest to the dilemmas of liberals confronted by a radicalism that they had neither the wish to stifle nor the will to embrace.

POLITICAL ACTIVISM ON CAMPUS

By the late fifties a new student left, some of it led by children of liberal and radical professionals, had begun to emerge on campuses. At Berkeley a student party named SLATE, dedicated to ending nuclear testing, capital punishment, Cold War rivalries, and other off-campus ills, began in 1957 to run candidates for student affairs elections. SLATE then incorporated civil rights into its agenda. Soon after, at the University of Wisconsin, students in history and the social sciences with a similar social and political profile launched an ambitious journal, *Studies on the Left*, committed to the "radicalism of disclosure." A visit to Berkeley in 1960 by Tom Hayden, editor of the *Michigan Daily*, the student newspaper at Ann Arbor, led on the University of Michigan campus to the formation of VOICE in imitation of SLATE. And there were stirrings of dissenting politics on other campuses as the Red-baiting era wound down in the late 1950s.

As early as 1960 Berkeley students delivered a blow for dissent when several hundred protested the hearings of the House Un-American Activities Committee (HUAC) in San Francisco. No group during that Cold War era more vividly represented than HUAC the general disregard for civil liberties. Police arrested many of the protesters or simply washed them down the steps of the city hall with fire hoses. The next day thousands of demonstrators returned to chant, "Sieg Heil!" and to bear witness that in California the days of unchallenged Red-hunting were over. *Operation Abolition*, a film put out by HUAC to show that these demonstrations had been the work of subversives, was so addlebrained that it strengthened the case of liberals against HUAC. *Operation Abolition* ultimately became a cult movie among campus sophisticates and dissenters.

BANNING THE LEAFLETS

In September 1964 Mario Savio, the son of a Roman Catholic machinist proud of his son's commitment to social justice, returned to campus after teaching at a freedom school in McComb during that greatest of Mississippi summers. Savio discovered that the campus authorities had declared off limits for advocates of civil rights and other causes a stretch of Telegraph

Avenue, the Bancroft strip, just outside the main gate to the Berkeley campus. For years the strip had been accepted as a place where students could hand out pamphlets, solicit names for petitions, and sign people up. But recently it had become identified with demonstrations against Berkeley and Oakland businesses that practiced discrimination. One of the demonstrators' chief targets was the *Oakland Tribune*, the East Bay newspaper published by William Knowland, the conservative United States Senator. The students' activities antagonized conservative university Regents and they pressured Berkeley to close the campus as a recruiting ground for activists and restrict student agitation in adjacent areas.

The ban set off a firestorm. Students who had taken on HUAC, Mississippi racists, Senator Knowland, and the East Bay business community were not about to be denied their rights by the likes of Clark Kerr. Groups representing SLATE members, anti-HUAC demonstrators, civil rights militants, and ordinary students, some of them conservative, protested the university's actions.

On September 29 the demonstrators defiantly set up tables on the Bancroft strip and refused to leave when told to do so. The next day university officials took the names of five protesters and ordered them to appear for disciplinary hearings that afternoon. Instead of five students, five hundred, led by Mario Savio, marched to Sproul Hall, the administration building, and demanded that they be punished too. Three leaders of the march were added to the list of offenders, and all eight were suspended.

REBELLION

The event that converted protest into rebellion occurred on October 1. As students arrived for classes that morning they were greeted by handbills declaring that if they allowed the administration to "pick us off one by one . . ., we have lost the fight for free speech at the University of California." Soon after, Congress on Racial Equality (CORE), Student Nonviolent Coordinating Committee (SNCC), the Du Bois Club,

Students for a Democratic Society (SDS), and six or seven other groups set up solicitation tables in front of Sproul Hall, the administration building. At 11:00 A.M. the assistant dean of students went up to the CORE table and asked Jack Weinberg to identify himself. Weinberg refused, and the dean ordered campus police to arrest him. A veteran of the civil rights movement, Weinberg went limp in standard civil disobedience mode when the guards carried him to a waiting car. Bystanders and observers quickly came to his rescue. In minutes hundreds of protesters, singing the civil rights anthem, "We Shall Overcome," and chanting, "Let him go! Let him go!" surrounded the car, preventing it from leaving to cart Weinberg off to security headquarters.

For the next thirty-two hours Weinberg and his police escort remained captive in the car while speaker after speaker climbed atop the vehicle to address the growing crowd. Savio, here and later the most civil of militants, removed his shoes so as not to damage the police car. He compared the protesters to Henry David Thoreau, who had briefly defied the authorities to protest the Mexican War that would enlarge United States slave territory. He was followed by other speakers, who were pelted with eggs and lighted cigarettes by about one hundred fraternity brothers and athletes.

The standoff ended with an agreement between Kerr and the warring parties that submitted to a committee of faculty, students, and administrators all issues of campus political behavior and turned over to an academic senate committee the question of suspending the eight students. Weinberg would be released without charges.

THE FREE SPEECH MOVEMENT

But the rebellion had only begun. A new organization, the Free Speech Movement (FSM), was formed with a large executive committee representing its constituent campus organizations. Despite the FSM's growing fear that the administration was not dealing with the students in good faith, the next few weeks were relatively quiet on campus. Yet incidents were accumulating that would provoke the students and help trip off another confrontation. Berkeley's chancellor Edward Strong refused a request that he reinstate the eight suspended students while the senate committee deliberated their fate. Kerr, who dismissed the FSM as "a ritual of hackneyed complaints," failed to realize that faculty, graduate students, teaching assistants, and undergraduates alike would perceive the issue as amounting not to how many restrictions had been removed but how many remained. Here the liberalism of the Berkeley administration, disposed to compromise, crashed head-on into the moral objectives of the student movement, as the liberalism of Kennedy and Johnson collided with the visionary purity of the civil rights activists.

The FSM proposed that the freedom defined in the First Amendment be considered the only guide to political activity on campus. Savio denounced a compromise reached by the senate committee for imposing prior restraint on student actions. On November 9, in defiance of the administration, Savio and his allies once again set up literature and solicitation tables. As a preliminary to disciplinary action, campus police took the names of seventy-five students supervising the tables. Now the student movement had antagonized not only the administration but also many of the more conservative student groups. On the other hand, it was gaining support among graduate students, many of whom were poorly paid, overworked teaching assistants. The graduate student organization declared that it would preside over tables. The administration, the TAs said, would not dare suspend them since their role was vital to the university's functioning. They were right. When almost two hundred graduate students set up tables nothing happened. Many undergraduates, deciding that the administration was choosing to pick only on the weak, shifted back to the FSM. What the incident really proved was that in a university essentially liberal in structure, students who were also teachers could undermine administrative authority.

On November 13 the dilatory liberals on the faculty senate committee finally made a report. Six of the eight suspended students should be reinstated; Savio and Art Goldberg should be kept on suspension for six weeks. By what one administrator described as a "mealy-mouthed liberal nondecision," Savio and Goldberg's sentences, however, should be made retroactive to the incident, more than six weeks in the past. With that problem out of the way, focus returned to the question of campus advocacy and solicitation for off-campus causes. The FSM leaders decided to confront the university's Board of Regents, who were scheduled to meet on the campus on November 20. To assure a good turnout, movement leaders prevailed on Joan Baez, the popular folk singer and a sympathizer with the FSM, to give a free concert during the meeting.

Baez brought out the crowd. Three thousand students gathered near Sproul during the Regents' meeting to listen to speeches. They then snake-danced their way to the west gate of the campus and sat on the grass to hear the singing and await the results of the meeting. The results disappointed most of Berkeley's students. No campus facilities could be used to further causes deemed "unlawful," and the Regents overruled the faculty and increased the punishments on Savio and Goldberg. The student militants could have wondered, like the SNCC workers in Mississippi in their dealings with liberal Democratic party forces in Washington: just what did the establishment want?

In the few remaining weeks of the semester, the FSM won increasing support on the Berkeley campus. Among administration blunders that brought the militants success was Chancellor Strong's against Savio and his associates for unlawfully hindering campus police from performing their duties. The graduate students decided to go on strike. On Wednesday, December 2, from four to five thousand people, spectators as well as FSM partisans, gathered around Sproul Plaza.

MARIO SAVIO SPEAKS FOR A GENERATION

In his indictment of the alienating, impersonal machine that he believed the university had become, Savio found his own authentic eloquence. Martin Luther King in the "Letter from a Birmingham Jail" had spoken of "direct action, whereby we would present our very bodies as a means of laying our case before the conscience of the . . . community." Now Savio announced:

> There's a time when the operations of the machine becomes so odious, makes you so sick at heart, that you can't take part; you can't even passively take part. And you've got to put your bodies upon the gears and upon the wheels, upon the levers, upon all the apparatus, and you've got to indicate to the people who own it that unless you're free, the machines will be prevented from working at all.

This is poetry that combines the exaltation of the civil rights movement with the splendor of the existential vision. It moved the listeners. And it placed the Free Speech Movement at about the point in the spectrum that much of the student left then spoke from: with no suggestion of violence, thinking of concrete change, its discourse as yet unthickened by dogmatic pseudorevolutionary verbiage.

Soon after the demonstration in the plaza, student supporters began to fan up and out across four floors of Sproul Hall singing "We Shall Overcome" and Bob Dylan's "The Times They Are-a Changin'." Savio, Weinberg, and others urged people on the plaza to join the sit-in. From one thousand to fifteen hundred went inside the building.

For a time it looked as though the administration would not act. Late that afternoon, university officials declared the building closed and sent employees home. As hours passed and nothing further happened, students inside Sproul relaxed. The FSM leaders designated separate areas and floors for special activities. There was a room for movies, another for a Spanish class, an area for quiet study, and a spot for square dancing.

THE POLICE MOVE IN

But off campus the forces of the establishment began to stir. To some observers the Berkeley rebellion seemed a heinous violation of the rules of university decorum, an outrageous defiance of rules and procedures by a privileged group of young people, beneficiaries of a generous taxpaying public. Around midnight the deputy district attorney of Alameda County told Governor Pat Brown in Los Angeles over the phone that "temporizing would only make the eventual blow-off more dangerous." Brown gave permission for the police to move in. Shortly after 2:00 A.M., six hundred California high-way patrolmen and Alameda County sheriff's deputies cordoned off Sproul Hall. In the middle of the night Chancellor Strong appeared with a bullhorn admonishing students to leave the building. The Free Speech leaders now began spreading the word that students should go limp to slow down the re-moval process. That way, the bust would still be going on at the time classes resumed in the morning, and uncommitted students, on the way to lectures and labs, would observe the cops manhandling their fellow students.

The police charged with resisting arrest any student who went limp. At first removals were gentle. Then, as the police tired, they became less careful. They twisted some arms and banged some students' heads on the stairs as they were dragged out. Such treatment by police of students was still an unfamil-iar experience. In all it took twelve hours to clear the building, but by midafternoon 773 of the occupiers had been arrested and booked for trespassing. Most were shipped off to the county prison farm at Santa Rosa, where a Black Muslim pris-oner, Huey Newton, looked on in amazement; all the students were released on bail the following day to return to Berkeley. It had been the largest mass arrest in the history of California.

The bust electrified the campus. By noon, when the police were still busy loading demonstrators into vans, as many as ten thousand people jammed the plaza, craning to see what was happening. It was a "sea of outraged faces," a witness noted. The crowd spilled over onto the roof of the Student Union across from the plaza and onto the adjacent playing fields. As they watched, many found FSM handbills thrust at them pro-claiming a universitywide strike to protest the tactics of the authorities.

THE FACULTY INTERVENES

That afternoon eight hundred faculty met at the invitation of Professor Seymour Lipset of the sociology department to consider the sit-in, the strike, and the police action. Much of the Berkeley faculty, especially in the humanities and the social sciences, was liberal, prepared to react against heavy-handed authority backed by the police. And faculty members were quite genuinely appalled at the violation of the haven for scholars to do their research, teaching, and learning. Students belong on campus; police do not.

The faculty recommended that all action pending against the students be dropped, that a faculty committee hear appeals from administration disciplinary decisions connected with political action, and that these appeals be final. It also approved a statement that no student be cited by the university for participating in off-campus political action. When a member of the bacteriology department condemned "the presence of the State Highway Patrol on the Berkeley campus," and demanded "the prompt release of the arrested students," the assembled professors cheered. After the meeting, many of the faculty headed for Alameda County Court House to post bail for the arrested students. For all the hesitancy of liberalism in the presence of agitation to its left, liberal faculty now acted in solidarity with their young academic offspring, and not least in parental solicitude for them.

THE STUDENTS STRIKE

Over the next few days the Free Speech leaders proved that they were capable not only of arousing strong feelings but of channeling them effectively. A Strike Central coordinated all strike activities and churned out thousands of flyers and handbills, many of them run off on the mimeograph machines of academic departments with friendly chairmen.

Support of the strike was not total. In the engineering, technical, and business fields, the turnout was weak. But in most disciplines teaching assistants and many faculty canceled classes to express support or to free themselves and their students to work for a solution of the crisis. Perhaps three-quarters of Berkeley's twelve hundred professors contributed to the strike by choosing not to hold classes.

Hoping to end confrontation, Kerr proposed a "new era of freedom under law." All Monday classes, he announced, would be canceled so that students, faculty, and administrators could meet at the Greek Theater to hear the proposals. Free Speech supporters came to the meeting in force along with many students sympathetic to the administration's tone of moderation. In all, by noon, sixteen thousand people filled the amphitheater.

Kerr read to the crowd a statement that dozens of department chairman had approved. It endorsed "orderly and lawful procedures" and condemned the sit-in as "unwarranted" and as likely to obstruct "fair consideration of the grievances brought forward by the students." The department chairmen then recommended against imposing further penalties on the arrested students and urged the resumption of classes forthwith.

During Kerr's reading, sections of the stands most sympathetic to the Free Speech Movement sometimes booed and jeered. Its leaders had demanded more: that the university intercede with the courts in favor of the arrested students. This display of feeling was a mere foretaste of what came at the end. Professor Robert Scalapino, chairman of the political science department, adjourned the meeting. Savio, who had been sitting in the press section just in front of the rostrum, walked onto the stage and attempted to speak. He never made it. Two campus guards immediately stopped him, pulled him from the rostrum, and dragged him backstage to an empty dressing room. Before a mass gathering in an open-air Greek theater, the free speech leader was being physically denied free speech. Even the most dogged parliamentarian might have allowed that granting brief access to the microphone would not have threatened good order at the event that was about over. There was nothing Kerr could do to remedy the situation. Pandemonium broke out. "Let him speak! Let him speak!" the crowd demanded. Savio was allowed to return to the stage, where he merely announced that his organization had scheduled a rally to follow immediately at Sproul Plaza. The students, he shouted, should leave "this disastrous scene and get down to discussing the issues."

THE ACADEMIC SENATE ACTS

The academic senate meeting the next day, December 8, was the zenith of the FSM arc. It was the largest turnout within memory for a body much given to routine discussion of courses, rules, and minor university policy. Outside, several thousand students gathered to listen to the deliberations carried from the room by loudspeakers.

The discussion revolved around the proposal of the senate's academic freedom committee endorsing the Free Speech Movement's basic positions on the disciplinary proceedings and the time, place, and content of speech and advocacy. In effect, it left the university authorities with only minimum traffic-cop powers to prevent physical disruption of the campus. A group of faculty moderates and conservatives led by Lewis Feuer of philosophy and Nathan Glazer of sociology opposed the committee's proposal. Feuer offered an amendment that committed the university to nonintervention in matters of speech and advocacy only when they were "directed to no immediate act of force and violence." He observed to his colleagues that the failure of the German universities in the early 1930s to insist that students be disciplined for off-campus attacks on Jews, liberals, and socialists had enabled Nazi students to destroy German freedom and prepared the way for the rise of Hitler. The liberals counterattacked. Owen Chamberlain, a physics Nobel Prize winner, deplored the paternalism implicit in the Feuer amendment. Others endorsed the right to mount boycotts, stage sit-ins, and establish picket lines to protest injustices in the outside community without university interference. Several noted that the students were watching them, a view that struck Feuer's party as a threat of mob violence if the faculty did not accept the original proposals.

The Feuer amendment was defeated 737 to 284; the vote on the original proposals carried 824 to 115. As the faculty filed out of the building the masses of student spectators greeted them with cheers and loud applause.

Within hours the Free Speech Movement called off the strike and issued a statement headed "Happiness Is an Academic Senate Meeting." Apparently Jack Weinberg's pithy slogan warning against trusting anyone over thirty had been proven wrong. The next day the movement won another victory. At the annual student government elections, SLATE, a part of the Free Speech coalition, swept into student government offices. Every SLATE candidate won. With double the usual voting turnout, the student government's existing conservative leadership was totally repudiated.

FREE SPEECH RETURNS TO THE BANCROFT STRIP

The eagerly awaited Regents' meeting on the 18th did not turn out well for the Free Speech supporters. The Regents refused to accept the academic senate's assumption of ultimate disciplinary authority over the students. The group did not pass on the substantive proposals of the senate's December 3 resolutions and promised only to appoint a committee from among its members to consult with students, faculty, and others to make recommendations at some later date. Pending completion of this process the existing rules would remain in force. But then fortunes shifted. On January 2 the Regents fired Chancellor Strong and as acting chancellor in his place appointed Martin Meyerson, dean of the College of Environmental Design. Meyerson had been a supporter of the Free Speech Movement, while Strong had been responsible for the Sproul bust. The Regents were clearly offering the student activists peace. Meyerson's first act was to accede almost totally to the Movement's fundamental demands. Henceforth students would be allowed to set up tables on the Bancroft strip and at other designated places on campus. Student organizations using these tables could receive donations, distribute literature, recruit members, and sell such items as buttons, pins, and bumper stickers.

The major issues now in the past, FSM was on its way to demise. Then, on March 3, a nonstudent drawn like others to the ferment at Berkeley sat down unobtrusively on the Student Union steps opposite Sproul. Possibly he uttered nothing; his sign, with two words, said it all: "F—— (verb)." A Berkeley city policeman reported it to the campus police, who promptly came and arrested the sign carrier. Again the campus flared.

A small demonstration at which speakers peppered their remarks with the word in question had led to eight arrests by campus police. But now the militants were divided. Radicalism had not yet reached the stage of verbal overkill that would characterize its violence-obsessed wing within the next few years; it was still deeply founded in the liberal academic traditions that respected precise and seemly speech. Savio, denouncing the new controversy for endangering rights hard-won, withdrew from FSM. The Filthy Speech Movement, as the latest agitation was termed, soon died.

"I am a human being," went in essence one of the more remembered student laments of the sixties: "I am not the sum of my data on a computer card. Treat me as well as you ask that our university cards be treated." Reduced to a message on signs that Berkeley students were carrying, the plea read: "I am a student. Do not fold, bend, mutilate, or spindle." If this is to be understood as a call for an education allowing for closer exchange between students and teachers, more respectful of students as potential contributors to the learning process, it is not only well phrased but eminently reasonable. But some student rebels came to want more: to equate their condition with that of a people for whom resistance is the only alternative to suffering. Modern life, in fact, had little to impose on American students that countless people during the Great Depression, or in any earlier time, would not have been envious to share. Savio, for all the sense of balance that distinguished him from many of his successors, announced that the police were "*family men, you know. They have a job to do. . . . Like Adolph Eichmann. He had a job to do. He fit into the machinery.*"

The equation of American cops with a bureaucratic Nazi architect of the Holocaust was a portent of the rhetorical confusions to come. Savio, moreover, had drawn parallels with the black freedom movement in the South. There was one critical respect in which the comparison was unsatisfactory: the nature of the enemy. At Berkeley, the antagonist was no more than the managerial liberalism of the university administration. Martin Luther King faced palpable evil; the students at Berkeley confronted paternalism.

Still, students were right to recognize that what happened, and happened to them, on their sheltered grounds belonged to the larger monstrous world. Their universities contributed to the institutions of wealth and war, which they were being trained as much to serve as to question. To acknowledge, without self-abasement, the extent to which they were privileged; to define, without self-dramatization, the ways in which they were exploited; to find the points of intersection between the cool critical methods of the academy and the impassioned issues of the time or any time: these requisites of a well composed student politics would have been difficult for the strongest of campus leaders to meet. Savio himself was hard-put to keep the balance.

CHAPTER 5

CONTEMPORARY FREE SPEECH CONTROVERSIES

AMERICAN
SOCIAL
MOVEMENTS

Free Speech and Sexual Harassment

DEBORAH ELLIS

In this excerpt from the symposium *Speech and Equality: Do We Really Have to Choose?*, Deborah Ellis, the legal director for the National Organization for Women Legal Defense and Education Fund (NOW LDEF), examines the problem of sexually harassing speech in the workplace. Ellis argues that since the First Amendment was designed to protect minority interests, it cannot be used to protect speech that sends a hostile message of exclusion. Ellis centers her analysis on a celebrated NOW LDEF lawsuit, *Robinson v. Jacksonville Shipyards*, in which employee Lois Robinson claimed that she was systematically targeted, harassed, and derided by her male coworkers. Ellis asserts that harassment serves to marginalize employees like Robinson, robbing them of traditional workplace remedies. Ellis points out that the workplace is a relatively private sector which does not qualify for the sweeping First Amendment protections accorded to traditional public forums, such as parks, street corners, or the steps of public buildings. Companies routinely restrict the speech of employees as part of conducting business. Accordingly, they should not tolerate messages of hostility and exclusion aimed at women unless they are prepared to relax all restrictions on speech in the name of free expression.

The conflict between speech and equality in the workplace has become a hot issue, at least in part because sexual harassment law is now addressing what I call the "second generation" employment discrimination cases. First generation cases focused on ending the *exclusion* of women from the workplace so that women could be hired or obtain promotions. Second generation cases address *conditions* in the workplace, thereby attempting to transform some of the male-centered norms that led to the exclusion. The goal is to create conditions in which true equality is possible, or in Title VII language, to change the "terms or conditions" of employment.[1]

In trying to accommodate values of speech and equality, we should focus not only on the different kinds of speech, but on the different forums where speech occurs—in this case, the workplace....

At least one civil liberties group, the American Civil Liberties Union (ACLU), works to expand workers' rights in *many* different contexts: from eliminating drug testing to penalties for conduct outside the workplace, such as smoking. Thus it is worthwhile to consider initially whether the principles of the First Amendment argue for the expansion of workers' speech rights, including the right to engage in offensive speech.

HARASSING SPEECH

Those who argue that harassing speech in the workplace should not be enjoined point out that part of the price of living in a free society is to tolerate speech that is highly offensive. Analogizing to the march of the Nazis through the Jewish suburb of Skokie,[2] they acknowledge that most people would not condone such speech, but point out that it is precisely speech "at the fringe" that needs protection. This is undoubtedly true. The First Amendment is not necessary to protect speech that the majority agrees with. Rather, like other provisions in the Bill of Rights, the First Amendment exists to protect minorities, which in this context are unpopular ideas.

Advocates for the primacy of free expression in the workplace go on to argue that women employees must accept the workplace as they find it and not be "politically correct" thought-police who tell other workers that their modes of ex-

1. Title VII of the Civil Rights Act of 1964 that prohibits employment discrimination based on race, color, religion, sex, or national origin. 2. The march was scheduled for May 1977 in the suburb of Chicago. The event never took place in Skokie. After winning his court battle, Nazi leader Frank Collin led a protest in Marquette park instead.

pression are offensive. Because under this analysis one solution for offensive speech is "more speech," women employees should instead respond by expressing their own ideas. For example, if confronted with demeaning photos of nude women, women could post demeaning photos of nude men (if one could find such photos).

An example of this view is a 1991 law review article entitled "Title VII As Censorship" by Kingsley Browne. In that article, Browne advocates that workplace speech expressing views about the qualities of certain groups, such as minorities or women, should be considered political speech in the same way that speech advocating nondiscriminatory treatment should be. Browne notes that courts have found that the more political the message, the more offensive it is. For example, the statement that "women belong in the bedroom and not the factory," is not only offensive but communicates a definite political viewpoint. Interestingly, Browne modifies his views somewhat for racial harassment cases, noting that the message in racial harassment cases is less ambiguous than that involved in the sexual context. The objectionable message in racial harassment cases is generally one of hostility and prejudice—racial slurs and epithets are common features—while in the sexual context, the message may be either hostile or sexual.

This distinction is illusory. The purported distinction illustrates [author and attorney Susan Deller] Ross's point that the term sexual harassment has disserved women by putting too much focus on sexuality. The real message in sexual harassment, like racial harassment cases, is one of exclusion. A case the National Organization for Women Legal Defense and Education Fund (NOW LDEF) brought in Florida, *Robinson v. Jacksonville Shipyards*, illustrates this point well.

THE *ROBINSON* CASE

In *Robinson*, NOW LDEF represented a woman welder, Lois Robinson, in a Title VII suit challenging the pornography and lewd comments she faced at a shipyard. Robinson is a first-class welder, one of the few women welders at the shipyard, and indeed one of the only female skilled craftsworkers in a workplace where "women craftsworkers are an extreme rarity." For example, in 1980, the shipyard employed two women and 958 men as skilled craftsworkers; in 1986, the percentages had improved to six women out of 846 men. The shipyard has never had a female supervisor.

After a trial, the district court cited many instances to support its findings of a hostile work environment. For example, Lois Robinson could not avoid the pervasive pornographic pictures in her workplace. They were posted where she worked, in the trailer where she picked up her tools; pictures were waved in her face and left on her toolbox. The pictures were explicit. They included photos of nude and seminude women in sexually suggestive or demeaning poses. One display was a dartboard with a woman's nipple as the bull's-eye; another was a woman's pubic area with a meat spatula pressed on it.

Some pictures were specifically targeted at Lois Robinson. For example, one picture that was waved in her face by a co-worker in an enclosed area where she worked was of a nude woman with long blonde hair wearing high heels and holding a whip. Robinson has long blonde hair and uses a welder's tool known as a whip. Not surprisingly, she felt particularly targeted by that picture.

Other women at the shipyards also experienced harassment by pornography. For example, two women were shown a picture of the infamous Long Dong Silver. In addition to the pictures, Lois Robinson also was subject to verbal harassment, such as a co-worker who said, "Hey pussycat, come here and give me a whiff." When Lois Robinson complained about these incidents, the complaint process became yet another occasion for harassment. Management told her that the shipyard is a "man's world" and agreed to remove only pictures of people having sex. In contrast, the foreman in charge of personnel testified at trial that he would probably throw any calendar with a picture of a nude man on it in the trash. Most telling, after a pornographic calendar on the shipyard trailer was removed in response to Robinson's complaints, a "men only" sign appeared on the trailer door. That sign declared explicitly what the pictures said implicitly.

This incident illustrates Ross's point that the term sexual harassment is a misnomer because sexual harassment in the workplace has little to do with sexuality and much to do with power. Women may no longer be explicitly barred from being welders, but harassment such as the pornography in *Robinson* communicates to women that they are not welcome in the male workplace.

VOICING A MESSAGE OF EXCLUSION

Why shouldn't workers be able to communicate such a message of exclusion? As Browne points out, such a message is political, and political expression has long been protected by First Amendment principles. For me, the key reason is the nature of the workplace. In addition to the reasons set forth by Ross, regulated speech in the workplace is permissible precisely because a workplace is a place for work, not a forum for the exchange of ideas. Employees of private employers already have the limited speech the employer chooses to bestow. Public employees have more rights, but even for them courts have recognized that concern for speech must be balanced against the employers' interest in ensuring the effective functioning of the office.

A central tenet of American free speech jurisprudence is the concept that the antidote to any speech with which one disagrees is counterspeech. As Justice [Louis] Brandeis wrote in *Whitney v. California*, the remedy for disagreeable speech "is more speech, not enforced silence." But in most workplaces, there is no realistic opportunity to counter with more speech because of the lack of significant numbers of women and the economic coercion of needing to earn a living.

Robinson illustrates why Brandeis's "more speech" antidote is unrealistic for most workers. At the shipyard, management had denied employees' requests to post political materials, advertisements, and commercial materials. It barred newspapers or other reading material due to safety concerns. Only one type of speech was allowed without prior approval: pictures of nude or seminude women.

A SPECTRUM OF PUBLIC AND PRIVATE FORUMS

I think it is useful to picture forums on a spectrum, with parks and other traditional public forums at one end and the workplace at the other. In between are forums that are more difficult to categorize. For example, a university traditionally has been a place of robust debate, yet it is also necessary for the university to afford equal educational opportunity. Another point on the spectrum is a shopping mall, a forum that should be categorized as public for speech purposes. In our mobile, consumer-oriented society, the shopping mall in many communities has become the true town square, and yet the U.S. Supreme Court has refused to recognize a right of free speech there.

Having said that the workplace is a forum where speech that excludes women should not be allowed, what should be the extent of permissible relief in a sexual harassment case? To remedy the discrimination at the shipyard, the trial judge in *Robinson* ordered a comprehensive remedy, including training of the shipyard workers, instituting policies and procedures to curb harassment, and a ban on posting pornography or bringing pornographic materials into the workplace. The ACLU filed an amicus brief in *Robinson* objecting to portions of this remedial relief on the grounds that it is overbroad, applies to material that is merely sexually suggestive, and bans nontargeted expressive activity. However, the NOW LDEF argues that the relief ordered must be viewed in light of the history of pervasive, deeply rooted sexual harassment at the shipyard and the broad principles of remedial relief in Title VII cases articulated by the Supreme Court in *Albemarle Paper Company v. Moody.* As the Supreme Court explained in *Albemarle*, courts have a "duty to render a decree which will so far as possible eliminate the discriminatory effects of the past, as well as bar like discrimination in the future."

Courts' broad remedial powers under Title VII justify some

infringement on constitutional rights if the remedy is narrowly tailored to serve a compelling government purpose. For example, courts have ordered remedial relief in hiring and promotion cases, such as a one-for-one promotion order, even when the Fourteenth Amendment equal protection rights of other employees are adversely effected. Moreover, the remedial relief ordered in *Robinson* must be considered in light of the shipyard's history of banning all public displays of expressive activity except sexual materials. There are no alternative remedies because by the management's own admission, the shipyard is large and hard to monitor.

As someone committed to feminism and civil liberties, I value both speech and equality. But to argue that offensive speech should not be subject to Title VII's prohibition of a hostile environment does not take sufficient account of the realities for women employees. Those who want to express a sincere view that women do not belong in the workplace can engage in other modes of communication, from talking to neighbors to writing letters to the editor to lobbying legislators. Some would say that those options are not sufficient, for much of social interaction in the modern era occurs at work, not in the mythical town square. But that fact must be balanced against the economic reality that women must work in order to provide for themselves and their families. In *Rabidue*, a Sixth Circuit case, the Court used the fact of pornography and other discrimination women face in society as a reason they should "tough it out" at work; the court said that Title VII was "not designed to bring about a magical transformation in the social mores of American workers." However, I think the *Robinson* court had the better view when it reiterated that "the whole point of the sexual harassment claim is that behavior that may be permissible in some settings can be abusive in the workplace."

The Problem of Limiting Pornography and Hate Speech

NICHOLAS WOLFSON

In this excerpt from his book *Hate Speech, Sex Speech, Free Speech*, Nicholas Wolfson describes how the right to free speech is being challenged by individuals who traditionally had supported it: feminists and members of minority groups. Many feminist critics argue that pornography and sexually harassing speech (especially in the workplace) perpetuate myths about the supremacy of men and the submissiveness of women. They worry that if such speech is not regulated, it will undermine the advances women have made in their struggle for equality. Minorities view hate speech the same way. Slurs aimed at ethnic minorities and homosexuals reinforce stereotypes and subvert the progress these groups have made toward the enjoyment of full civil rights. These critics argue that the right to free speech was not meant to protect those who would oppress others through false, misleading, and derogatory speech. While Wolfson sympathizes with minority causes, he disputes the notion that restricting speech benefits anyone. He criticizes the notion that speech should be rationed according a kind of quota system, with each ethnic group receiving a certain amount of representation in various media. Such limits, he argues, will interfere with that natural flow of ideas that society depends on for social progress.

Nicholas Wolfson is a law professor who served as branch chief, special counsel, and assistant director at the Security Exchange Commission in Washington, D.C. He is author of numerous books and scholarly articles in the fields of corporate law, securities regulation and free speech.

The traditional, liberal, civil rights position on free speech issues is under powerful assault in the academy. Old allies in the liberal alliance have parted company. Feminist and African-American intellectuals, as well as many white male scholars, now question the old notion that strong free-speech protection is not only defensible but offers the best route to a just society. Rather, the new critics of the old liberal verities argue on a number of fronts that the strong version of free speech disenfranchises blacks, women, gays, and lesbians.

Two kinds of speech are singled out. First, there is hate speech. It is difficult to define this category precisely, but it generally includes offensive speech directed at minorities. In its most vulgar form, it includes the racial and sexist epithet, such as "kike" and "fag." At a more subtle level, or so it is argued, it includes books, cinema, and television images that demean a minority. For example, many African-Americans view the American classic *The Adventures of Huckleberry Finn* as an example of hate speech. (Some Jews view portions of the New Testament as hate speech directed at Jews, the alleged killers of God; although no one argues for its censorship, many call for clarification.)

Hate speech is criticized as lacking any of the elements that warrant constitutional protection. Hence, scores of universities have enacted speech codes that ban hate speech. It is depicted as emotional speech without intellectual content. Worse, the new critics of the First Amendment argue that hate speech is false, lacking any basis in science or enlightened culture. Worst of all, such speech degrades the objects of abuse, silences them through fear, does them psychological damage, and creates a smarmy and nauseating culture that harms women and minorities.

Another criticized category of speech (and image) is pornography. Modern feminist scholars have eloquently argued that pornography is a zero-value form of expression that maintains patriarchal dominion over women in Western (and in fact all) cultures. Indeed, they argue, it is not expression at all but an act of violence against women that silences and harms them. Even pornographic art, cinema, or television that reflects talent or even genius is so harmful that it should be censored.

The eloquent criticisms of hate speech and pornography are based in large measure on alleged disparities in speech power between women and minorities on one hand, and white males in the modern age of corporate giants and billionaire entrepreneurs on the other. Constitutional scholars have begun to pay attention to the problem of speech inequality. While traditional civil libertarians continue to find their inspiration in the nearly absolute language of the First Amendment, other scholars are increasingly looking to the equality language of the Fourteenth Amendment or to general principles of egalitarianism.

Feminist theorists argue that American society is so inherently sexist that, as we have indicated above, the constitutional protection of speech actually serves to subordinate women. Two frequently cited examples of speech-as-subordinator are pornography and verbal sexual harassment in the workplace, such as festooning shops or offices with photographs of women in sexually provocative poses. Feminists consider these to be methods of warfare by men against women, because they treat women as sexual objects, reflecting both the subordinate position of women and the preservation of male dominance. Many view these activities as political speech inherent in the war of the sexes, in which women are often the losers.

In this view, sexist talk is a weapon used by men in a ceaseless gender war. Sexist talk is a deeply structured and fundamental, albeit perverse, means by which men define their status and, indeed, their meaning. As Nancy S. Ehrenreich put it, "Under this view, [a female worker's] insistence that [a male worker] refrain from displaying pornography would have prevented him from following a fundamental tenet of his group's philosophy and undermined the sense of identity, of maleness, that the act of displaying pornography affirms." Limiting his freedom would assist women's political battle for power but necessarily limit his power and that of the male class.

Feminists argue that pornography and sexually harassing words in the workplace enforce men's dominance and efforts to subordinate women. As Kathryn Abrams eloquently argues, "Pornography on an employer's wall or desk communicates a message about the way he views women, a view strikingly at odds with the way women wish to be viewed in the workplace.... It may communicate that women should be the objects of sexual aggression, that they are submissive slaves to male desires."

Abrams refers to empirical investigations indicating that "women are more likely to regard a sexual encounter, *verbal* or physical, as coercive." She further asserts that "men are less likely to regard such conduct as harassing, and more likely to view it as a flattering reflection on their physical or personal attributes." She concludes that male judges may reach results that do not chill "verbal sexual abuse ... and dissemination or display of pornography." To the argument that courts should adopt an attitude that "reflects both men's and women's views of sexually oriented conduct in the workplace," Abrams responds that equal perspectives will perpetuate the subordination of women.

Minority rights theoreticians also make this inequality argument with great vigor. Constitutional law scholars have written in recent years about the alleged inability of African-Americans, Hispanics, gays, and lesbians to engage effectively in the so-called "free market of ideas" because of the imbalance of power inherent in a racist society. Hence, many colleges and universities have enacted speech codes that attempt to redress the imbalance by banning offensive racist, sexist, and homophobic speech.

Any effort to ration speech, however, carries with it extremely serious consequences. In the first place, there are some obvious problems. Who is to ration? How can we trust the rationers? The risk of bias is enormous. Politicians and bureaucrats cannot be trusted to allocate speech to people or causes they dislike. Conflicts of interest arise. Government officials arc not likely to apportion "speech chits" to individuals who may expose government peccadillos. The dominant political forces of the moment will seldom allocate speech in a manner that will threaten them.

How could we ration? What standards could we use? African-Americans, for example, might demand that 12 percent of every opinion section of a newspaper be devoted to African-American causes. Hispanics might demand a quota based upon their own percentage of the population; religious fundamentalists might make a similar demand; and feminists might demand a percentage devoted to their causes. Affirmative action and quotas would radically alter the essence of speech and the speech dialectic. Speech is dynamic; it moves and convinces in mysterious and unpredictable ways. Speech is the essential attribute of humanity, close to the core of human autonomy. A cabining and leveling of speech might reduce and diminish the human spirit.

Nevertheless, certain feminist and minority spokespersons fear failure of their cause without a sort of affirmative action for "proper speech" and limits on speech that allegedly drowns out feminist and minority voices (even though their ideas have triumphed in key establishments). A remarkable *New York Times* article by Alessandra Stanley describes the almost absolute dominion of liberal political voices in Hollywood. She reports how directors and actors with conservative viewpoints must hide their opinions or risk almost certain industry retribution. The same, as many assert, is often true in our prestigious universities.

Feminist and minority speech has had a dramatic effect on American mores. The intellectual redoubts—elite universities, the media, and the cinema—are clearly in the hands of liberal and left-wing men and women. On the other hand, religious and political conservatives are outraged at the imbalance in favor of liberal and radical visions of economics, gender, and race in cinema, television, and the university.

Through novels, cinema, television, and scholarly research,

free speech in the capitalistic West has transformed the societal vision of women's roles. Men in the workplace, blue collar and white, have begun to internalize a proper vision of women, racial minorities, gays, and lesbians. Free speech, as currently defined, has been a weapon for feminism, and for gay and lesbian rights. Subjugated groups will restrict it only at great cost. Restrictions may create resentment and anger; they may prolong the battle for equality rather than shorten it.

Of course, women, racial minorities, and the gay and lesbian communities are impatient with the pace of progress. Some believe that the 1992 Republican presidential convention demonstrated the power of feminist, gay, and lesbian-bashing. The 1994 Republican sweep aroused great fear in liberal groups. (On the other hand, it has encouraged conservative groups who fear the liberal "bias" of the media and Hollywood). But these sentiments do not necessarily militate for censorship. The world is surfeit with examples of groups impatient with the progress of certain ideas and the possibility of rapid peaceful change who sought victory not by speech but by censoring it. History teaches that unacceptable levels of government coercion and force lie in that direction.

But this view of progress may be Panglossian [i.e. all is for the best in the best possible of worlds]. There are no guarantees that speech we despise will fail. The cruel dilemma is that left unfettered, certain ideas triumph, and some perspectives will see them as bad ones. Speech is fluid. It moves with an unpredictable dynamic and is inherently incompatible with balance. Ideas are born, develop, and dominate, or languish and perish, as part of a complex interaction of culture and dialectic that cannot be easily described or reduced to a cookbook formula. Speech rationing would attempt something like a fix or stasis in the dialectic based upon a belief in a "just" balance. The fix would be governed by a belief in a "rational" and "truthful" end or goal for society. Given the unpredictable and sometimes dangerous dynamic of speech, the issue is then the following: Why should we permit hateful or sexually offensive speech?

Regulating Speech on College Campuses

TIMOTHY C. SHIELL

Timothy C. Shiell is associate professor of philosophy at the University of Wisconsin–Stout and editor of the volume *Legal Philosophy: Selected Readings*. In this excerpt from his book, *Campus Hate Speech on Trial*, Shiell tries to find a middle ground between advocates of college speech codes and critics of such regulations. Shiell agrees that broad speech codes threaten free speech. On the other hand, he believes that individuals should be protected from a hostile environment created by inappropriate conduct related to hate speech. Shiell prescribes a narrow speech code that distinguishes speech from conduct. He bases his solution on five lessons he has learned from analyzing speech codes. First, the "hostile environment" standard created by federal antidiscrimination laws is the best ground for regulating hate speech. Second, the hostile environment standard must be defined carefully and precisely. Third, speech codes cannot be enacted simply to further personal opinions or ideology. Fourth, free speech is a fundamental right and an aid to furthering equality. Finally, universities have a unique tradition and important responsibility for promoting free speech. By paying attention to these five points, Shiell argues that hate speech can be regulated without endangering speech as a whole.

In the present state of the art, there is no satisfying resolution to this dilemma [of regulating hate speech]. There simply is no philosophical, legal, political, or social scientific standard or standards that will put the issue to rest. But assuming

Timothy C. Shiell, *Campus Hate Speech on Trial*. Lawrence: University Press of Kansas, 1998. Copyright © 1998 by University Press of Kansas. All rights reserved. Reproduced by permission.

the five lessons I drew in the previous section are on the right track, I propose the following framework.

First, universities should begin by recognizing that formal proceedings accompanied by sanctions (whether mandatory "reeducation" seminars, required apologies, suspensions, expulsions, etc.) must be a small part of the overall effort to ensure equal opportunity. If a university genuinely hopes to make progress in the fight for equality, it must focus on educational and economic measures. The sanctions imposed by a speech code, as even advocates realize, will do little by themselves to foster a concern for equality and respect for racial, religious, gender, and ethnic differences. Which is more effective in the long run: developing grassroots support for racial equality at Central Michigan or having a speech czar dictate that the word "nigger" cannot possibly have a positive meaning? A proactive educational and economic stance should yield better results in the long term than a reactive punitive stance.

In fact, the short-term thinking represented by acceptance of makeshift punitive speech codes should be replaced by long-term thinking aiming at educating not just students, but the American population in general. Higher education has not been very successful at this, and it appears that the growing gap between higher education and the rest of society has enabled some opportunists to mount a powerful attack on higher education in the 1990s. Too often these opportunists are able to exploit the fracture amongst university personnel caused by the hate speech debate and cast the privileged as browbeaten underdogs on American campuses. Universities must make stronger efforts to teach all Americans to understand and appreciate both equality and free speech. Instead of paying J. Donald Silva and his lawyers $230,000 for an illegal hostile environment prosecution, the University of New Hampshire could have funded a number of campus educational forums, community outreach programs, scholarships for minorities or women or the financially needy, and the like.

Second, universities should charge those responsible for enforcing any speech policy with scrupulously protecting free speech rights and not merely with vigorously promoting equality. This means, amongst other things, that universities must ensure that due process rights are protected. Proponents of equality will simply continue to draw the fire of many who would be their allies if they continue to encourage double standards, the presumption that the accused are guilty the moment a complaint is filed, and the belief that consensual sex is "really" coerced or otherwise involuntary. An affirmative action officer, who typically has little or no training in free speech law or academic freedom, is probably not the best person to enforce a speech policy. Universities will continue to get hammered in the courts if their affirmative action officers and presidents go before the court and admit they have no principled way to distinguish illegal verbal harassment from merely offensive word. . . .

It is in virtue of this fact that I suggest, thirdly, that universities design policies that focus on conduct, not speech. In trying to get students to be more tolerant of different cultures and ideas, we set a poor example when we fail to tolerate different cultures and ideas! We must tolerate ideas that we hate (to paraphrase Justice Holmes), but we need not tolerate conduct that violates clear-cut rights. . . .

Compare: It is not illegal to desire a rich man's property; it is illegal to steal a rich man's property; and depicting or advocating the forcible confiscation of a rich man's property is regulated (e.g., a communist's "manifesto" is protected speech, whereas a rioter's call to storm the fences is not: the difference, roughly speaking, is in the targeted nature and the harm caused). Again: It is not illegal to desire to have sex with a minor; it is illegal to engage in sex with minors; and depicting or advocating sex with minors is subject to regulation (e.g., novels and news reports generally are protected, whereas photographs of sex with minors are not: the difference, roughly speaking, is in the targeted nature and the harm caused). Ideas in and of themselves, however hateful, are protected; actions are not; and the expression of the idea is regulable under certain narrowly defined conditions.

The fact is, the "accepted" view of free speech, in spite of its many recent critics, is still essentially the accepted view.... The line demarcating speech and conduct is not set in stone, to be sure, but to abandon this distinction—that is, to treat all speech as conduct and all conduct as speech—would be nonsensical. Since the First Amendment protects speech, if all conduct is really speech, then all conduct would be protected; yet, if all speech is really conduct, then the First Amendment protects nothing. The First Amendment becomes meaningless in either case. Edward Eberle notes in his analysis of *R.A.V.* [Supreme Court decision in *R.A.V. v. St. Paul* (1992)] that

> the difference between speech and conduct, sometimes stark, sometimes obscure, marks the emerging frontier of public discourse jurisprudence. Since one can view all words as "simultaneously communication and social action," the distinction between speech and conduct may be less intuitive than it seems. Still . . . in the end, we must make sense of our world. Thus, in First Amendment law, even though "every idea is an incitement to action"; the Court ultimately has wisely decided that "the line between what is permissible and not subject to control and what may be subject to regulation is the line between ideas and overt acts."

Thus it is that courts, in spite of their sympathy with the victims of hate speech and their acceptance of the goal of equality (conservative critics of equality correctly point out that equality has been and is enforced mostly by the judiciary), have not been convinced by the arguments of campus speech code advocates. Judge [Avern] Cohn in *Doe* [*Doe v. University of Michigan* (1995)]: "While the court is sympathetic to the University's obligation to ensure equal educational opportunities for all students, such efforts must not be at the expense of free speech." Judge [Robert] Warren [1991] in *UWM Post* [*UWM Post v. Board of Regents of the University of Wisconsin System*]: "The problems of bigotry and discrimination sought to be addressed here are real and truly corrosive of the educational environment. But freedom of speech is almost absolute in our land." And Justice [Antonin] Scalia in *R.A.V.*: "Let there be no mistake about our belief that burning a cross in someone's yard is reprehensible. But St. Paul has sufficient means at its disposal to prevent such behavior without adding the First Amendment to the fire."

Nor should the courts be convinced by the arguments of campus speech code advocates. The first thing to suffer in American society when greater speech restrictions are accepted will be the effort to attain equality. The powers that be in society at large have little interest in greater equality. It does not take a lot of insight to see that enforcers of the status quo will turn any speech restrictions to their advantage. If egalitarians fear that antiegalitarians have too loud a voice today, wait until broader speech restrictions are adopted. I have little doubt the speech of feminists, including Catharine MacKinnon, critical race theorists, homosexuals, "revisionist" historians, and other social critics will fare considerably worse if the doors are opened to greater censorship of ideas and their expression.

I am not suggesting that universities do not or should not regulate any speech. In fact, no one I know involved in the debate holds that position. I agree with [University of Chicago law professor] Mary Becker that

> the boundaries of every academic conversation, as well as many assessments of academic quality, turn on questions of content, viewpoint, and ideology. More pointedly, unspoken rules and understandings about what speech is high quality permeate university life—and these turn on content and viewpoint. These assessments, grounded as they inevitably are in traditional notions of what a discipline is about, count as "truth," and what methods are valuable, hurt many newcomers to the university communities. . . . Indeed the value of their speech could lie precisely in its divergence from university standards. . . . Yet no court would entertain a constitutional challenge [to these speech regulations] under the free speech clause.

The question is, Why are these speech regulations permissible (generally speaking) and hate speech regulations not permissible (generally speaking)? Becker maintains that it is purely a matter of tradition, but her analysis is too quick. The differences between the "regulations" she mentions and hate speech regulations are not obvious when you lump everything together; but when you examine them individually, relevant differences begin to appear. For example, although it is not hard to see how a university could avoid enforcing hate speech rules, it is impossible to see how a university could avoid any content or viewpoint judgments in hiring and firing decisions. Courts have balked at enforcing campus hate speech codes because there are other reasonable avenues (in particular, educational ones) for dealing with it. What is the alternative to hiring and firing on some kind of content and viewpoint? Even the most lazy and incompetent person could claim wrongful firing because the university would simply be "prejudiced" against the lazy and incompetent viewpoint. Should the university strive for neutrality in its hiring and firing decisions by using a coin? Heads you're hired, tails you're fired. That's not even neutral, I guess, because it is "dualistic" and punishes those who have a more pluralistic viewpoint. Is not being hired for a job because of content (they need a medievalist, he's a Far East scholar) really comparable to being suspended because one compares homosexuality to bestiality? Is Becker utterly ignoring academic freedom, the right of the professor to determine within professional standards which course materials are most appropriate, the right of a law school to hire more critical race theorists than racists? The freedom she implicitly attacks is the very freedom that enables her to publish her article in a book, attend academically sponsored conferences on her favored topics, and so on. Is Becker failing to address the distinctions [Justice] Scalia makes when he addresses content-neutrality in *R.A.V.*?

Becker takes an even more serious turn for the worse when she begins to attack binding judicial review (the right of courts to strike down legislation as unconstitutional without any recourse for the legislature to overturn the court's decision by, e.g., a supermajority vote). Her reasoning is this: Since the hate speech regulation movement has failed to convince judges of the justness of their cause, they should undermine the judge's ability to make binding law and work through legislatures to enact their hate speech codes. It is a turn for the worse for an obvious reason: If binding judicial review is undermined and legislatures are free to enact majoritarian desires, is it likely that the majority will enact the desires of critical race theorists, academic feminists, gay and lesbian radicals? To suppose this cuts against the very foundation of those views, in which each views itself as a victim of widespread social oppression. What is much more likely is that the backlash against egalitarians would be even more fierce—consider, for example, what is happening with affirmative action in recent years. Those who regard it as an essential component of greater social equality do not have any majority willing to support them. [Former executive director of the American Civil Liberties Union (ACLU)] Ira Glasser has put the point more succinctly:

> The attempt by minorities of any kind—racial, political, religious, sexual—to pass legal restrictions on speech creates a self-constructed trap. It is a trap because politically once you have such a restriction in place the most important questions to ask are: Who is going to enforce them? Who is going to interpret what they mean? Who is going to decide whom to target? The answer is: those in power. And what possible reason do minorities have to trust those in power?

This is not to suggest that egalitarians should not try to influence legislators, city council representatives, and other officials. Rather, it is to say that they shouldn't put all their eggs in one basket. The best hope for egalitarians is education, political agitation, and recourse to the courts to enforce constitutional guarantees when necessary. To attack judicial review as a whole because it fails to deliver one desired outcome is shortsighted in ignoring the host of desirable outcomes it has delivered and continues to deliver. Becker's argument reveals the (implausible) lengths to which advocates of broad campus hate speech codes will go to attain their ends and shows in yet another way how some "liberal" advocates of broad campus speech codes draw upon old-line "conservative" arguments.

Thus, rather than lump all speech restrictions into one basket or attack judicial review as Becker does in order to push for a broad hate speech code, I suggest that universities regulate only hate speech that targets a specific individual or individuals in a captive-audience context (regardless of the race, gender, religions, etc., of the speaker and hearer), is intended to cause harm to that individual or individuals, is clearly unrelated to any legitimate academic purpose, and is repeated (or, in an individual instance, sufficiently egregious) or done in conjunction with illegal conduct. Speech code advocates get a lot of mileage out of discussing cases that involve conduct violations. They characteristically mix in violent conduct with wounding words. But illegal conduct is not at issue in the hate speech debate. The hate speech debate cases strictly speaking involve only pure speech incidents. And those should be narrowly defined. Thus, a male student who yells "nice tits" to a female student across an open-air campus area (as in one of the Wisconsin cases) should not be hauled before a speech czar to face formal discipline even if he intended to embarrass rather than compliment her. Instead, the woman, friends, and bystanders should express their disapproval of the remark. Resident directors should hold open forums to discuss such incidents. Faculty should bring it up in relevant courses. Interested parties should write letters to the campus newspaper to express their opinions about the incident. The student newspaper, the faculty senate, the university president can voice an opinion. The ways this comment can be informally dealt with are limited only by the imagination. On the other hand, a male student who says "nice tits," "I want to f——— you," and other sexually explicit remarks to a female student every time he sees her before and after class, even after she has made clear that this attention is unwanted and has taken reasonable steps to avoid his harassment, and who is in fact interfering with her academic progress should be subject to some kind of sanctions. Targeted, intentional, repeated verbal abuse serving no legitimate academic purpose is identifiable, and its regulation is consistent with controlling court decisions.

A policy focused on conduct and targeted, intentional, repeated verbal abuse is unlikely to have any chilling effect on legitimate speech. Students should not have a hard time recognizing the difference between (a) vigorous, even heated, debates over sexual orientation, affirmative action, racism, welfare, belief in God, and other issues and (b) targeted, intentional, repeated verbal abuse. They will be free to pin up posters and invite onto campus speakers that other groups find highly offensive; but they will not be free to threaten or "feel up" people. Faculty should not have a hard time recognizing the difference between (a) using a sexual example in philosophy class to explain, say, Plato's or J.S. Mill's distinction between qualitatively superior and inferior pleasures and (b) using non-course-related sexual jokes and banter to discourage women from taking or succeeding in a required chemistry course. Faculty should be free to champion ideas hated by others and vigorously attack views cherished by others; but they should not be free to conduct campaigns of terror or intimidation or bar students from the classroom simply because the student disagrees with the professor's opinion, for example, that lesbians make the best parents.

Some extremists, perhaps Kingsley Browne, may object that my policy permits punishment of pure speech without any "conduct" elements. In assessing this objection, we must be cognizant of two points. First, regardless of my opinion or the extremist's opinion or anyone else's opinion about the punishment of pure speech without any conduct elements under the hostile environment standard, the Supreme Court's ruling in *Harris* [*Harris v. Forklift Systems, Inc.* (1943)] permits this and is, at least for now, controlling precedent. Egregious pure speech cases must be dealt with by universities on pain of civil damages, at least in employment contexts. Second, the regulation of pure speech without any conduct elements accepted by the Court in *Harris* is essentially correct (even Antonin Scalia accepted the court's position that conduct elements are not necessary where the speech is sufficiently egregious). The reason for this is that through the interpretation of our Constitution in dozens of court cases and enactment of many federal, state, county, and city laws we have decided that an individual's equality rights and interests are important enough to his or her life prospects to deserve protection. The fact that the philosophical basis for this collective decision is not settled (nor ever likely to be settled) is not particularly troublesome to pragmatically minded folk, since the reality is that equality in the workplace is shaped by speech and not just by conduct, and any public policy that denies that is unrealistic. It doesn't follow, of course, that broad regulation of speech is therefore justified, since our speech interests must be attended to as well.

To my mind, the problem with *Harris* is not that it allows for regulation of pure speech in egregious cases, it is the problem Scalia notes in his separate concurrence: The Court needs to set clearer guidelines in place to help us distinguish legitimate from illegitimate claims of hostile environment. . . . For example, such policies must be content-neutral and provide enough clarity to avoid (minimize?) arbitrary enforcement. My policy is content-neutral in applying to all harassing speech, not merely such speech as applied to certain protected classes, and is unlikely to be arbitrarily enforced if monitored by a diverse committee governed by due process guidelines and educated in free speech doctrine. Campus policies and enforcement must be sensitive to these and many other concerns . . . captive-audience contexts, fair notice, due process, and more. I think [editorialist and columnist] Linda Seebach said it well: "Universities need to have harassment policies, of course, but they also need the backbone to tell complainants, gently but firmly, when they don't have a case."

If the five lessons I have drawn are substantially correct, those who advocate a more restrictive or less restrictive code than the one I propose here have a heavy burden of argument to bear. A more restrictive code will run afoul of established free speech doctrines, and a less restrictive code will run afoul of established equality doctrines. It will be my pleasure, of course, to refine and correct this proposal in light of future developments. One of the difficulties in taking a position in this debate is seeing clearly where the agreements and disagreements are, given how much the two sides seem to talk past one another. Yet there is perhaps less disagreement than one might suppose. Tom Foley, the Ramsey County, prosecutor who argued on St. Paul's behalf in the *R.A.V.* case, has since said, "My position was that most speech is protected, but that if speech reaches the criminal threshold it is not. For instance, if the skinheads in *R.A.V.* had decided to march down the street in a parade burning a cross, I would have reluctantly agreed with the majority that this was protected speech. I argued that if there is a threat to a particular individual, then it is not protected." I agree. And would add that R.A.V. was charged by the Justice Department under different statutes, convicted, and required to serve two years in a juvenile workhouse for his crime, not his speech. We must take hate crimes seriously and not dismiss all cases as innocuous pranks or overactive hormones or mere ignorance or isolated incidents. Howard Erhlich and others have done extensive research documenting ethnoviolence. This plague must be addressed, and universities should not hesitate to impose available sanctions on hate criminals. We should also take hate speech seriously and not dismiss it as mere pranks, overactive hormones, or the like either. Universities should not hesitate to deal with serious hate speakers and provide solid educational strategies for fostering understanding. What they must not do is commit blunders that end up trivializing real harassment.

Before concluding, I want to address a final complaint some readers have expressed, namely, that my proposal is contradictory. On the one hand, I criticize speech codes and the hostile environment standard in drawing my "lessons," while on the other hand, I advocate a hostile environment speech code in my modest proposal. What gives? What gives is the contradiction. There is no contradiction in accepting two competing values (in this case, freedom and equality) and attempting to find a workable balance between them. . . .

Accepting the two propositions "Freedom of speech is an important value" and "equality of opportunity is an important value" is not contradictory since there can be two important values, and rejecting broad campus speech codes while accepting a narrow one is not contradictory since there are clear reasons to reject the former but embrace the latter. The criticisms of speech codes and the hostile environment standard I endorse are not so weighty as to rule out every possible speech regulation. If they were, we would have to abandon *all* speech regulations, including those on child pornography, bribery, quid pro quo harassment, and such; and no serious participant in the hate speech debate believes all speech regulations must go. The criticisms are, however, weighty enough to require the careful qualifications I have outlined here. Rather than get caught up in debate about logical consistency here, we ought to focus on the relative value of the competing ideals and search for practical ways to resolve the tensions between them. This is what public policy analysis essentially is. . . .

The campus hate speech debate is not dead and is not just of historical interest. The issues, unresolved as they are, are upon us today, demanding our attention and action. We want the guilty to be punished and the innocent to be left alone. We demand immediate solutions. We demand protection of our constitutional rights. We demand both freedom and equality. We want people to be viewed and treated according to their merit and not their skin color or genitalia or ethnic heritage or religious belief. We want people to be free to challenge the status quo. Yet, we can't have it all. There is no unassailable "middle ground" or "higher ground" upon which to resolve these issues. Any policy will leave something to be desired. But we must still set the best policy we can within current limitations and larger strategies and goals. . . .

When we put hate speech on trial, the stakes are high: no less than social justice and our national identity. How we deal with dissent, intolerance, threats, harassment, and offensive ideas concerns two of our most cherished ideals. Let us not abandon one for the other, but continue to search for ways we can more effectively realize both.

Free Speech
and the Internet

A freelance writer living in Washington, D.C., Joshua Micah Marshall is the author of the *Talking Points Memo*, a contributing writer for the *Washington Monthly*, and a columnist for the *Hill*. Marshall graduated from Princeton University and earned a doctorate in American history from Brown University. His articles on politics and culture have appeared in the *American Prospect, Blueprint,* the *Boston Globe,* the *Columbia Journalism Review,* the *Los Angeles Times,* the *New Republic,* the *New York Post,* the *New York Times,* the *Washington Monthly*, and various other publications. He has appeared on *Crossfire, Fox and Friends, Hannity and Colmes, Hardball,* and many other television and radio talk shows.

Written after the Supreme Court had struck down the Communications Decency Act for violating the First Amendment, this article explores less overt methods of Internet censorship. According to Marshall, the advent of content filtering and the Platform for Internet Content Selection has shifted the role of censorship from the sender to the receiver. These technologies allow Internet users to filter out materials they find offensive, but they also present hidden dangers to free speech.

W hen the Supreme Court overturned the Communications Decency Act (CDA) [in 1997], its decision seemed to put to rest much of the controversy over internet free speech. But there are now a host of more limited efforts afoot to prune back the range of internet content and limit access to various kinds of online material. Such technical innovations as "content filtering" and "censor-ware" make it

Joshua Micah Marshall, "Will Free Speech Get Tangled in the Net?" *The American Prospect*, January/February 1998, p. 46. Copyright © 1998 by The American Prospect, Inc., 5 Broad St., Boston, MA 02109. All rights reserved. Reproduced by permission.

CONTEMPORARY FREE SPEECH CONTROVERSIES • 197

possible for individuals, employers, internet service providers, and others to block out selected portions of the online world. While the CDA's criminal penalties for publishing "indecent" material made an easy mark for free speech advocates, these new forms of control pose more subtle and incremental threats—and should force us to confront whether keeping the government out of the censorship business will be sufficient to assure freedom online.

The new world of online media is inevitably changing the terms of debate about freedom of speech and of the press. Words, ideas, and images are being liberated from their original connection to such physical objects as books, papers, magazines, and photographs, and the costs of copying and transmitting information are dropping sharply. Just what constitutes "publishing," for instance, becomes blurred when books, articles, and even casual notes can be distributed to the entire world, instantaneously and at negligible cost. Much of the difficulty of crafting good public policy for the Internet stems from the fact that the Net removes all the incidental and often overlooked ways in which we have traditionally used physical space to segregate and restrict information. Consider the fact that Playboy magazine is behind the counter and not on the magazine rack at the local convenience store, or that certain subterranean activities can only be found in the seedier sections of our central cities. If these tacit ways of organizing information are to be reproduced on the Internet, they must be explicitly reconstituted. But often these barriers can only be rebuilt with meddlesome and obtrusive changes in the way the Web works.

CONTENT FILTERING

Much of the debate over how to reconstitute the old barriers and regulate the flow of online information centers on "content filtering" and something called PICS (the Platform for Internet Content Selection). PICS originated in the minds of the men and women who designed the World Wide Web. While Congress was hashing out what would become the

Communications Decency Act, a group of internet policy planners began to formulate a system that would allow individual users to decide what could and could not appear on their computer screens. Rather than banning information at the "sending" end, internet users would be able to block offensive material at the "receiving" end. Everybody could then carve out his or her own zone of comfort on the Internet, with just the right mix of Puritanism and prurience. It was an ingenious solution—a kinder, gentler version of the CDA. It would assuage the fears of parents, conciliate free speech advocates, and short-circuit the political argument for a broad regime of internet censorship.

The PICS project was coordinated and directed through the World Wide Web Consortium, an independent body that has taken a leading role in formalizing standards and protocols for the Web, with support from many of the biggest internet industry companies. The designers went to great lengths to make the system unobjectionable to both civil libertarians and those who wanted to limit the circulation of indecent material. In fact, their literature betrays an almost quaint sensitivity to the theory and language of multiculturalism. They designed PICS not as a set of ratings or categories but as a format for devising a variety of different ratings systems, each reflecting different cultural and political perspectives. To understand the distinction, consider the difference between a word processing format like Microsoft Word and the infinite variety of documents that one could author in that format. PICS is not a rating system; it is a format that can be used to create many different rating systems.

PICS envisions at least two basic models in which rating systems might operate. The first—and conceptually more straightforward—is self-rating. Publishers of Web sites rate their own material, alerting viewers to coarse language, nudity, or violence. Publishers would choose whether to rate their sites and, if so, what ratings system to use. PICS would also allow third-party rating. Different organizations or companies could set up "rating bureaus" that would rate sites according to their own political, cultural, or moral standards. Thus the Christian Coalition might set up its own rating bureau, as could the National Organization for Women. Individual users could then decide whether to filter material using the voluntary self-ratings or subscribe to a rating bureau that suited their personal sensibilities.

Upstream Filtering

Given the obvious similarities, many have compared PICS to an internet version of the much-touted V-chip [which enables owners of televisions equipped with the technology to block reception of programs they find objectionable]. But the V-chip analogy is only partly correct, and the differences are telling. The weight of the argument for the content filtering approach is that individuals decide what they will and will not see. But PICS-based content filtering is actually much more flexible and scalable than this standard description implies. There are many links in the information food chain separating your personal computer from the source of information. And what you see on the Internet can potentially be filtered at any of those intermediate points. You can block material at your computer, but so can libraries, your employer, your internet service provider, your university, or even—depending on where you live—your nation-state. With the V-chip you control what comes on your television set. But with PICS the choice may not be yours.

There are already a host of new software products on the market that allow this sort of "upstream" content filtering. They are being introduced widely in the workplace and, to a lesser degree, in schools and libraries. This so-called internet access management software makes possible not just filtering and blocking but also detailed monitoring of internet usage. It can monitor what individual users view on the Web and how long they view it. It can even compile percentages and ratios of how much viewing is work related, how much is superfluous, and how much is simply inappropriate. These less savory uses of the technology won't necessarily be used. But the opportunities for abuse are obvious and they reach far beyond issues of free speech into elemental questions of personal privacy.

The other problem with PICS is more subtle and insidious. You often do not know just what you are not seeing. Because of a perverse but seemingly inevitable logic, companies that provide content filtering or site blocking services must keep their lists hidden away as trade secrets. The logic is clear enough. The companies expend great resources rating and compiling lists of prohibited sites; to make those lists public would divest them of all their value. But whatever the rationale, this practice leads to numerous tangled situations. Public libraries that have installed site blocking software are in the position of allowing private companies to determine what can and cannot be viewed in the library. Even the librarians don't know what is blocked and what is not.

INDIRECT CENSORSHIP

The possible integration of search engine technology and PICS-based rating holds out the prospect of a Web where much of the material that would not appear on prime-time television just slips quietly out of view. Even more unsettling, many internet search engine companies—with a good deal of prodding from the White House—have announced plans to begin refusing to list sites that will not, or cannot, rate themselves. Again, the implications are far-reaching. With the increasing size and scope of material on the Web, most people use search engines as their gateway to finding information online. Not being listed is akin to having the phone company tell you that you are welcome to have as many phone numbers as you like but no listings in the phone book. This is one of the ways in which "voluntary" self-rating can quickly become a good deal less than voluntary. There are also bills pending before Congress that would either mandate self-rating or threaten sanctions for "mis-rating" internet content. This is the sort of creeping, indirect censorship that makes PICS so troubling.

One of the compensations of real-world censorship is that school boards and city councils actually have to ban unpopular books and look like fools doing it. The crudeness and heavy-handedness of the state's power to censor is always one of the civil libertarians' greatest advantages in battles over the banning and burning of books. But content filtering makes censorship quiet, unobtrusive, and thus all the more difficult to detect or counter. It is difficult to quantify just what is different about the new information technology. But the essence of it is an increasing ability to regulate the channels over which we communicate with one another and find out new information.

To all these criticisms the creators of PICS say simply that they and their technology are neutral. But this sort of "Hey, I just make the guns" attitude is hardly sufficient. To their credit, they also point to the more positive uses of content filtering. And here they have a point. In its current form the Internet is a tangled jumble of the useful, the useless, and the moronic. PICS could help users cut through the clutter. Topic searches could become more efficient. In one oft-cited example, content filtering could allow internet searches for information about a particular medical condition that would produce only material from accredited medical organizations. Of course, the question then becomes, who accredits? There are standards of authority and discrimination we will gladly accept about information for treating breast cancer that we would never accept if the topic is, say, art or political speech. And in any case none of these potentially positive uses negate, or really even speak to, the reality of possible abuses.

THE APPEAL OF CENSORSHIP

This new debate over content filtering has sliced apart the once potent coalition of interests that banded together to defeat the Communications Decency Act. One of the striking features of the anti-CDA fight was how it lined up technologists, civil libertarians, and major corporations on the same side. What became clear in the aftermath, however, was that companies like Microsoft, Netscape, and IBM were not so much interested in free speech, as such, as they were in preventing government regulation—two very distinct concepts that we now tend too often to conflate.

In fact, the seamless and adaptable censoring that makes civil libertarians shudder is precisely what makes it so attractive to business. Businesses do not want to refight culture wars in every locale where they want to expand internet commerce. If parents from the Bible Belt are afraid that their children will find gay rights literature on the Web, they won't let them online to buy Nintendo game cartridges either. The same logic is even more persuasive when commerce crosses international borders. International internet commerce is widely seen as one of the most lucrative prospects for the internet industry, and much of that trade would take place with countries that either do not share American standards of cultural permissiveness or that routinely censor political material. Content filtering will let American companies sell goods to China over the Internet without having to worry that pro–Tibetan independence Web sites will sour the Chinese on the Internet altogether. Content filtering allows us to carve the Internet up into countless gated communities of the mind.

These concerns about "cyber-rights" can seem like overwrought digital chic—an activism for the affluent. And often enough, that is just what they are. But it is important to take a broader view. Today the Internet remains for most a weekend or evening diversion and only relatively few of us use it intensively in the workplace. But the technologies and principles that we formulate now will ripple into a future when the Internet—and its successor technologies—will be more and more tightly stitched into the fabric of everyday communication. In a world of books and print, the "Government shall make no law" formulation may be adequate. But in a world of digitized information, private power to censor may be just as deleterious as public power, and in many respects may be more so.

FREE EXPRESSION AT RISK

There is also an unfortunate convergence between this growing power of nongovernmental censorship and the declining value of open expression as a positive social ideal. In a political climate such as ours, which is generally hostile to government power, a subtle and perverse shift can take place in our understanding of the First Amendment and the importance of free speech. We can begin to identify the meaning of free speech simply as a restriction on governmental power and lose any sense that free speech has value on its own merits. One might say that it is the difference between free speech and free expression, the former being narrow and juridical, based largely on restrictions on government action, and the latter being a more positive belief not in the right but in the value of open expression for its own sake. We seem to be moving toward a public philosophy in which we would shudder at the thought of government censoring a particular book or idea but would be more than happy if major publishing companies colluded together to prevent the same book's publication.

Our political and cultural landscape is replete with examples. We see it in support for the V-chip, government's strong-arming of TV networks to adopt "voluntary" ratings, and in the increasingly fashionable tendency for political figures to shame entertainment companies into censoring themselves. The sort of public shaming of which Bill Bennett [author and former Secretary of Education] has made a career has a very good name in our society, and too few speak up against it. The move to rate television programming may well be benign or, at worst, innocuous in itself. But it points to a broader trend for government to privatize or outsource its powers of censorship. This sort of industry self-regulation is said to be voluntary. But more and more often it is "voluntary" in the sense that Senator John McCain must have had in mind when he threatened to have the Federal Communications Commission consider revoking the broadcasting licenses of NBC affiliates if the network did not agree to adopt the new "voluntary" TV rating system.

The idea that there will be a great multiplicity of rating systems may also be deceptive. Despite the possibility of an infinite variety of rating systems for a multitude of different cultural perspectives, everything we know about the computer and internet industries tells us that pressures lead not toward multiplicity but toward concentration. Aside from Microsoft's various anticompetitive practices, basic structural forces in the computer and software industries make it likely that we will have one or two dominant operating systems rather than five or six. The Web browser market has followed a similar trend toward consolidation. There would likely be a greater demand for a diversity of options in the market for content filtering and site blocking services. But the larger, overarching economic pressures—and the need to create vast economies of scale—would be simply overwhelming. Effectively rating even a minute portion of the Web would be an immense undertaking. The resources required to rate the Web and constantly update those ratings could be recouped only by signing up legions of subscribers. Far more likely than the "let a hundred flowers bloom" scenario is one in which there would be a few large companies providing content filtering and site blocking services. And these would be exactly the kind of companies that would become the targets of crusading "family values" politicians trying to add new candidates to the list of material to be blocked.

THE FIRST AMENDMENT, UPDATED

The novelty of this new information technology calls on us to think and act anew. We cannot now foresee what changes in technology are coming or what unexpected implications they will have. What is clear, however, is that there is no easy translation of real-world standards of intellectual freedom into the online world. Our current conceptions of First Amendment rights are simply unequal to the task. It is easy enough to say that the First Amendment should apply to cyberspace, but crude applications of our current doctrines to the online world involve us in unexpected and dramatic expansions and contractions of intellectual freedoms and free speech. In the architecture of the new information economy, private power will have a much greater and more nimble ability to regulate and constrict the flow of information than state power will. Taking account of this will mean updating both the jurisprudence and the public philosophy of free speech rights. Much like the law of intellectual property, public policy toward free speech must undertake a basic reconsideration of the values it seeks to protect and the goals it seeks to serve.

Partly this will mean focusing more on the goals of First Amendment freedoms and less on the specific and narrow mechanics of preventing government regulation of speech. It may even mean considering some informational equivalent of antitrust legislation—a body of law that would intervene, not to regulate the content, but to ensure that no private entity or single corporation gained too great a degree of control over the free flow of information. What it certainly does mean is that we must abandon that drift in public policy that allows government to outsource its power to censor under the guise of encouraging industry self-regulation. Government may not be fully able to alter some of the pernicious directions in which information technology is evolving —and it may be good that it cannot. But government can at least avoid policies that reinforce the negative tendencies. "Voluntary" industry self-regulation should really be voluntary and we should inculcate within ourselves—and particularly our policymakers— a critical awareness of the implications of new technologies. Whatever the merits of creating PICS and the infrastructure of content filtering, now that it exists we must be vigilant against potential abuses. We should make critical distinctions between the narrow but legitimate goals of content regulation—like providing mechanisms for parents to exercise control over what their children see—and the illegitimate uses to which these technologies can easily be applied.

There are many ways in which we can subtly adjust the law of intellectual property, civil liability, and criminal law to tip the balance between more or less restrictive regimes of free speech, privacy, and individual expression. The federal government might limit the ability to claim intellectual property rights in lists of blocked sites. Such a policy would limit the profitability of commercial ventures that compiled them. We can also limit, as much as possible, internet service providers' liability for what material flows through their hardware. This would remove one of the incentives that they would have for filtering content before it reached the individual user. Yet another tack is to rethink the civil liabilities we impose on employers when rogue employees download obscene or conceivably harassing material on their computer terminals. This, again, would remove at least one of the rationales for pervasive content filtering in the workplace. Sensible public policy can be devised to safeguard the values of an open society in the information age. But too often we are letting technology lead public policy around by the nose.

What we need is a wholesale reevaluation of our collective attitudes toward the meaning and value of free speech and the role it plays in our society. Though we strain mightily to avoid government censorship, there is little public commitment in our society today to a culture of free expression on its own merits. Public calls from Bill Bennett to shame media companies into "doing the right thing" are widely acclaimed. Political leaders too often take a wink-and-a-nod approach when private bodies take on the censoring role that government itself cannot. But the myopic focus on government as the singular or most significant threat to free speech rests on a basic misreading of our history. In America, the really pointed threats to free speech and free expression do not come from government. They never have. They have always come from willful majorities intent on bullying dissenters into silence. The new information technology and content filtering make that even more feasible than it has been in the past. And that is the problem.

CHRONOLOGY

1789

James Madison offers an amendment to the Constitution that states, "The people shall not be deprived or abridged of their right to speak, to write, or to publish their sentiments; and the freedom of the press, as one of the great bulwarks of liberty, shall be inviolable."

1791

Virginia ratifies the first ten amendments to the Constitution, making them law. The final version of the First Amendment states, in part, "Congress shall make no law . . . abridging the freedom of speech, or of the press."

1798

Congress passes the Sedition Act, calling for the punishment of any person who would "write, print, utter or publish . . . any false, scandalous and malicious writing or writings against the government of the United States."

1862

After the outbreak of the Civil War, President Abraham Lincoln issues a proclamation calling for the arrest of anyone "affording aid and comfort to Rebels."

1863

Ohio congressman Clement L. Vallandigham is arrested, tried, and convicted for speaking out against Lincoln and the war.

1868

Congress passes and the states ratify the Fourteenth Amendment. The Supreme Court later rules that the amendment's due process clause safeguards "the liberty of the press, and of speech . . . from invasion by state action."

1919

In *Schenck v. United States*, the U.S. Supreme Court rules that the First Amendment does not protect expression that incites a crime. The opinion also suggests that laws restraining speech must be narrowly tailored to serve compelling interests of the government.

1942

U.S. Supreme Court rules in *Chaplinsky v. New Hampshire* that "insulting or 'fighting' words—those which by their very utterance inflict injury or tend to incite an immediate breach of the peace"—are not protected by the First Amendment.

1943

In *West Virginia State Board of Education v. Barnette*, the U.S. Supreme Court holds that students cannot be forced to say the Pledge of Allegiance.

1948

The American Library Association adopts the Library Bill of Rights, which states in part, "Libraries should challenge censorship in the fulfillment of their responsibility to provide information and enlightenment."

1951

In *Dennis v. United States*, the U.S. Supreme Court rules that the Smith Act, which makes it a crime for any person "to advocate the overthrow or destruction of the Government of the United States by force or violence," does not violate the First Amendment.

1953

The American Library Association and the American Book Publishers Council adopt "The Freedom to Read Statement," which states, in part, "It is the responsibility of publishers and librarians, as guardians of the people's freedom to read, to contest encroachments upon that freedom by individuals or groups seeking to impose their own standards or tastes upon the community at large."

1957

In *Roth v. United States*, the U.S. Supreme Court holds that "obscenity is not within the area of constitutionally protected speech or press."

1959

In *Smith v. California*, the U.S. Supreme Court strikes down a Los Angeles city ordinance that makes the possession of obscene material a crime even if the defendant has no knowledge as to the contents of the material.

1964

Students at the University of California at Berkeley protest against a college administration policy banning leaflets that promote off-campus events and causes. The series of protests would become known as the Berkeley Free Speech Movement.

1971

In *New York Times Co. v. United States,* the U.S. Supreme Court vacates an injunction that prevented the *New York Times* from publishing the Pentagon Papers, secret documents relating to the Vietnam War that were stolen from the Department of Defense.

1973

In *Miller v. California* and *Paris Adult Theatre I v. Slaton,* the U.S. Supreme Court reaffirms that obscenity is not protected speech. In *Miller,* the Court announces a new three-part test for juries to follow in determining obscenity.

1981

In *Haig v. Agee*, the U.S. Supreme Court rules that former government employee Philip Agee does not have a constitutional right to disclose information about intelligence operations.

1982

The U.S. Supreme Court rules in *Board of Education v. Pico* that books cannot be banned from school libraries on a partisan political basis or even to uphold orthodox beliefs.

1984

In *City Council v. Taxpayers for Vincent*, the U.S. Supreme Court upholds a Los Angeles city ordinance forbidding the posting of signs on public property.

1989

Holding that burning the American flag in protest is "expressive conduct protected by the First Amendment," the Supreme Court in *Texas v. Johnson* overturns Gregory Johnson's conviction for desecrating the flag.

1996

Congress passes and President Clinton signs the Communications Decency Act (CDA), making it illegal to post indecent and patently offensive material on the Internet.

1997

The Supreme Court strikes down the Communications Decency Act.

1998

Congress passes and the president signs the Child Online Protection Act (COPA). The law prohibits commercial Web sites making material considered "harmful to minors" available to children sixteen and under.

2000

In *City of Erie et al. v. Pap's A. M., tdba "KANDYLAND,"* the Supreme Court upholds a city ordinance that forbids public nudity, including nude dancing. Congress passes the Children's Internet Protection Act (CIPA), which bars public libraries from receiving federal assistance for Internet access unless they install filtering software designed to block obscene or pornographic images.

2002

In *Ashcroft v. American Civil Liberties Union*, the U.S. Supreme Court upholds the constitutionality of the community standards test of the Child Online Protection Act to identify what material is harmful to minors.

2003

In *United States v. American Library Asssociation, Inc.* the U.S. Supreme Court upholds the constitutionality of the Children's Internet Protection Act. In *Virginia v. Black*, the U.S. Supreme Court upholds a Virginia law banning cross burning that is intended to intimidate.

2004

The U.S. Supreme Court hears arguments in *Ashcroft v. American Civil Liberties Union* to determine the constitutionality of the Child Online Protection Act.

FOR FURTHER RESEARCH

Books

Ellen Alderman and Caroline Kennedy, *In Our Defense: The Bill of Rights in Action.* New York: Avon Books, 1991.

David S. Allen and Robert Jensen, eds., *Freeing the First Amendment.* New York: New York University Press, 1989.

Stanley C. Brubaker, *The Bill of Rights: Original Meaning and Current Understanding.* Ed. Eugene W. Hickock. Charlottesville: University Press of Virginia, 1991.

David Burner, *Making Peace with the Sixties.* Princeton, NJ: Princeton University Press, 1996.

Francis Canavan, *Freedom of Expression: Purpose as Limit.* Durham, NC: Carolina Academic Press, 1984.

Frede Castberg, *Freedom of Speech in the West: A Comparative Study of Public Law in France, the United States, and Germany.* Oslo, Norway: Oslo University Press, 1960.

Michael Kent Curtis, *Free Speech, "The People's Darling Privilege": Struggles for Freedom of Expression in American History.* Durham, NC: Duke University Press, 2000.

Deborah Ellis, "Workplace Harrassment," in *Speech and Equality: Do We Really Have to Choose?* Ed. Gara LaMarche. New York: New York University Press, 1996.

Stanley Fish, *There's No Such Thing as Free Speech and It's a Good Thing, Too.* New York: Oxford University Press, 1994.

Douglas M. Fraleigh and Joseph S. Tuman, *Freedom of Speech in the Marketplace of Ideas.* New York: St. Martin's, 1997.

John Frohnmayer, *Out of Tune: Listening to the First Amendment.* Golden, CO: Fulcrum, 1995.

Mike Godwin, *Cyber Rights: Defending Free Speech in the Digital Age*. New York: Times Books, 1998.

Kent Greenwalt, *Speech, Crime, and the Uses of Language*. New York: Oxford University Press, 1989.

George Hay, *Two Essays on the Liberty of the Press*. New York: De Capo, 1970.

Nat Hentoff, *The First Freedom: The Tumultuous History of Free Speech in America*. New York: Delacorte, 1980.

———, *Free Speech for Me—but Not for Thee*. New York: Harper-Collins, 1992.

P.G. Ingram, *Censorship and Free Speech: Some Philosophical Bearings*. Burlington, VT: Ashgate, 2000.

Milton R. Konvitz, ed., *Bill of Rights Reader*. Ithaca, NY: Cornell University Press, 1973.

Duane Lockard and Walter F. Murphy, *Basic Cases in Constitutional Law*. Washington, DC: CQ Press, 1992.

John Stuart Mill, *The Basic Writings of John Stuart Mill: On Liberty, the Subjection of Women and Utilitarianism*. New York: Modern Library, 2002.

William H. Rehnquist, *All the Laws but One*. New York: Alfred A. Knopf, 1998.

Robert D. Richards, *Freedom's Voice: The Perilous Present and Uncertain Future of the First Amendment*. Washington, DC: Brassy's, 1998.

Bruce W. Sanford, *Don't Shoot the Messenger: How Our Growing Hatred of the Media Threatens Free Speech for All of Us*. New York: Free Press, 1999.

Timothy C. Shiell, *Hate Speech on Trial*. Lawrence: University Press of Kansas, 1998.

Rodney A. Smolla, *Free Speech in an Open Society*. New York: Alfred A. Knopf, 1992.

Richard W. Steele, *Free Speech in the Good War*. New York: St. Martin's, 1999.

Samuel Walker, *In Defense of American Liberties: A History of the ACLU*. New York: Oxford University Press, 1990.

James Weinstein, *Hate Speech, Pornography, and the Radical Attack on Free Speech Doctrine*. Boulder, CO: Westview, 1999.

Nicholas Wolfson, *Hate Speech, Sex Speech, Free Speech*. Westport, CT: Praeger, 1997.

Web Sites

American Civil Liberties Union (ACLU), www.aclu.org. The ACLU is a national organization that works to defend Americans' civil rights. It opposes all forms of censorship and seeks to protect the rights of individuals to free speech and free press.

American Library Association (ALA), www.ala.org. The ALA provides leadership for the development, promotion, and improvement of library and information services and the profession of librarianship. Its Office for Intellectual Freedom is dedicated to furthering the concept of intellectual freedom and educating librarians and the general public about the nature and importance of intellectual freedom in libraries.

Constitutional Rights Foundation (CRF), www.crf-usa.org. CRF is a nonprofit, nonpartisan, community-based organization dedicated to instilling in American youth a deeper understanding of citizenship through values expressed in the Constitution and its Bill of Rights, and to educate them to become active and responsible participants in society.

Morality in Media, Inc. (MIM), www.moralityinmedia.org. MIM opposes what it considers to be indecent material in broadcasting—especially pornography. It works to educate and organize the public in support of strict decency laws and has launched an annual "Turn Off the TV" day to protest offensive television programming.

National Coalition Against Censorship (NCAC), www. ncac.org. NCAC opposes censorship in any form, believing it to be against the First Amendment right to freedom of speech. It works to educate the public about the dangers of censorship, including censorship of violence on television and in movies and music.

National Coalition for the Protection of Children and Families, www.nationalcoalition.org. The coalition is an organization of business, religious, and civic leaders who work to eliminate pornography. It encourages citizens to support the enforcement of obscenity laws and to close down pornography outlets in their neighborhoods.

INDEX

Abermarle Paper Company v. Moody (1975), 177

Abrams, Kathryn, 182

Adams, John, 16, 117

Albany Argus (newspaper), 132

Alberts v. California (1957), 96

Alexandrinus, Dionysius, 24–25

Alien and Sedition Acts (1798), 115–21
see also Sedition Act

American Civil Liberties Union (ACLU), 18, 173
fight for free speech by, 140–55

Anti-Federalists, position of, on bill of rights, 57–58

Antony, Mark, 11

Aptheker, Herbert, 157

Areopagitica (Milton), 13

Asbury, Herbert, 149

association, freedom of, 154

Bache, Benjamin Franklin, 117

Baer, Elizabeth, 17, 77, 79

Baez, Joan, 162

Baldwin, Roger, 140, 141, 144, 145, 152

Barron v. Baltimore (1833), 72–73

Beauharnais v. Illinois (1952), 101

Becker, Mary, 189–90

Bennett, Bill, 204

Bentham, Jeremy, 35

Berkeley Free Speech Movement, 156–64
academic senate response to, 167–68
faculty response to, 165
student strike in, 165–67

Berns, Walter, 63

Bill of Rights
English, 13–14
free press provisions in original draft of, 56

Blackstone, William, 13, 29
on liberty of the press, 33–34

Boos v. Barry (1988), 108

Bork, Robert, 61

Boston, censorship in, 149–50
challenge to, 143–44

Brandeis, Louis, 73
on "clear and present danger" test, 148
on remedy for disagreeable speech, 176

Brandenburg v. Ohio (1969), 107

Brennan, William, Jr., 98–99, 102

Brown, Pat, 164

Browne, Kingsley, 174

Browning, Orville H., 125

Brubaker, Stanley C., 53

Bryan, William Jennings,

142, 143
Burner, David, 156
Burnside, Ambrose, 17, 122, 125
Butterworth, John C., 144

Campus Hate Speech on Trial (Shiell), 185
Caplinsky v. New Hampshire (1942), 107
Caset, John Michael, 149
Castberg, Frede, 69
censorship
  indirect, of Internet, 201–202
  previous restraint as, 70–71
Censorship in Boston (ACLU), 150–51
Chafee, Zechariah, Jr., 55, 147, 149, 150
Chamberlain, Owen, 167
Charles I (king of England), 49
Chase, Samuel, 62
Chicago Tribune (newspaper), 134–35
Cicero, 11
Cincinnati Commercial (newspaper), 132
Civil War, 17
  struggle for free speech during, 122–39
"clear and present danger" test, 81
Cohn, Avern, 188
college campuses
  regulation of speech on, 185–96
  see also Berkeley Free Speech Movement

Commentaries on the Laws of England (Blackstone), 29
Communications Decency Act (CDA), 19, 197
community standards, on obscenity, 97–100
Congress, U.S., Frankfurter on role of, 88–91
Constantine (Roman emperor), 11
Constitution, U.S., 14
  see also Bill of Rights; First Amendment; Fourteenth Amendment
Contraception (Stopes), 153
Cox v. New Hampshire (1941), 72
Curtis, Michael Kent, 122

Darrow, Clarence, 142, 143
David v. Massachusetts (1897), 71
Democracy in America (Tocqueville), 67
Dennett, Mary Ware, 151–53
Dennis v. United States (1951), 23–24, 82, 96
  concurring opinion in, 83–94
Detroit Free Press (newspaper), 132–33, 134
Dewer, John, 152
Doe v. University of Michigan (1995), 188
Douglas, William O., 95
Douglass, Frederick, 129–30

Ehrenreich, Nancy S., 181
Eisenhower, Dwight D., 102
Ellis, Deborah, 172

English Bill of Rights
(1689), 13–14
Espionage Act (1917), 17, 77
Euripides, 10

Federalist Papers, The, 58, 67
Federalists
  Alien and Sedition Acts
    and, 115
  position of, on bill of rights,
    57–58
Feuer, Lewis, 167
First Amendment
  application of, to states,
    72–73
  basis of, 24
  Internet as challenge to
    philosophy of, 205–207
  original intent of, 53–63
    modern interpretation
      and, 63–65
  protects offensive speech,
    102–13
  provisions of, 45, 69, 75
  ratification of, 15
  restriction of pornography
    violates, 95–101
*First Freedom: The Tumultuous
History of Free Speech in
America, The* (Hentoff), 115
Fiske, Harold, 148–49
flag burning, as protected
  speech, 102–13
Flynn, Elizabeth Gurley, 152
Foley, Tom, 195
Fourteenth Amendment, 73,
  147
  banning of hate
    speech/pornography and,
    181

remedies for rights
  infringement and, 178
Frankfurter, Felix, 16, 82,
  144, 145
Freedom of Speech in the West
  (Castberg), 69
free speech
  ACLU fights for, 140–55
  in ancient world, 10–11
  boundaries of, 51–52
  in early America, debate
    over, 14–17
  extending definitions of,
    18–19
  judicial vs. legislative
    remedy for pursuit of, 19
  limits of, 44–52
  Madison's interpretation of,
    64
  setting limits on, 74–75
  social progress and, 12–14
  struggle for, during Civil
    War, 122–39
  wartime restraints on, 16–17
*Free Speech, "The Peoples
Darling Privilege"* (Curtis),
  122

Galileo Galilei, 12
Geiger, Joseph, 126
Gelasius (pope), 11
Gitlow, Benjamin, 18
*Gitlow v. People of the State of
  New York* (1925), 18, 55, 65,
  73, 141, 146–47, 148
Glasser, Ira, 191
Glazer, Nathan, 167
Goldberg, Art, 162
Goldman, Emma, 152, 153
Gregory (pope), 12

Grosjean v. American Press Co. (1936), 69, 70–71

habeas corpus, 124–25, 136
Hague v. Committee for Industrial Organization (1939), 71
Hamilton, Alexander, 14, 116
  on Bill of Rights, 58
  on Constitution as bill of rights, 58
Hammurabi (Babylonian king), 10
Hand, Augustus, 152
harassing speech, 173–74
Harris v. Forklift Systems, Inc. (1943), 193–94
Hascall, Milo, 126
hate speech
  problem of limiting, 179–84
  regulation of, on college campuses, 185–96
Hate Speech, Sex Speech, Free Speech (Wolfson), 179
Hay, George, 16–17, 47
Hayden, Tom, 158
Hays, Arthur Garfield, 143, 149
Hentoff, Nat, 115
Holmes, John Haynes, 150
Holmes, Oliver Wendell, Jr., 73, 77, 147
  on meaning of free speech, 55, 65
House Un-American Activities Committee (HUAC), 158
Hughes, Charles Evans, 70, 154, 155

Hurtado v. California (1884), 73

incitement, doctrine of, 77–81
In Defense of American Liberties: A History of the ACLU (Walker), 140
Internet, free speech and, 197–207

Jefferson, Thomas, 14, 115–16
  on Alien and Sedition Acts, 120
  on control of speech by states, 16, 86
Johnson, Gregory Lee, 102, 103–13
Joyce, James, 153
judicial review, 88
Judiciary Act (1798), 62

Kaul, Donald, 13
Kerr, Clark, 157, 160, 166
Knowland, William, 159
Kunz v. New York (1951), 72

Largent v. Texas (1943), 72
Leavitt, Humphrey H., 128
Left-Wing Manifesto, The (Gitlow), 18, 146
Legacy of Suppression (Levy), 56
Leopold, Nathan, 142
Levy, Leonard, 56, 60
liberty
  civil, 32
  limits of, 38–39
  natural, 31

as protection against
  tyranny, 36
social, 35–42
Licensing Order by
  Parliament (1643), 12, 13
Lincoln, Abraham, 17, 131
  on arrest of Vallandigham,
    136–37
  on election during Civil
    War, 138–39
  on suspension of habeas
    corpus, 124–25, 135–36
Lipset, Seymour, 165
Loeb, Richard, 142
Lothrop, George V.N.,
  133–34
Lovejoy, Owen, 123–24
Luther v. Borden (1849), 125
Lyon, Matthew, 118–19

Madison, James, 14–15,
  44–52, 56
  on Alien and Sedition Acts,
    120–21
  on government's right of
    self-preservation, 84
  interpretation of free
    speech by, 66
Making Peace with the Sixties
  (Burner), 156
Malcolm X, 157
Married Love (Stopes), 153
Marshall, John, 93
Marshall, Joshua Micah, 197
McCain, John, 204
McCormick, Robert, 154
Means, John A., 131
Meikeljohn, Alexander, 150
Meletus, 10
Mencken, H.L., 149

Meyerson, Martin, 168
Mill, John Stuart, 20, 35
  on liberty of the press,
    41–42
Milner, Lucille, 141
Milton, John, 12–13, 23
  on censorship, 26–28
Moses, 10

Near, Jay, 154
Near v. Minnesota (1931), 69,
  154–55
Nelles, Walter, 147
Newton, Huey, 164
New York Times (newspaper),
  183
*New York Times Co. v. United
  States* (1971), 18

obscenity
  community standards and,
    97–100
  lack of clear test for, 96–97
  Supreme Court's definition
    of, 100
On Liberty (Mill), 35
Operation Abolition (film), 158
opinion, freedom of, 39–41
Ovid, 11

Patterson v. Colorado (1907), 80
People v. Wepplo (1947), 96
PICS (the Platform for
  Internet Content
  Selection), 198–202
Plato, 10
Pollak, Walter, 146–47
Pontius Pilate, 11
pornography
  problem of limiting,

179–84
restriction of, violates First
Amendment, 95–101
press, liberty of the
common law understanding
of, 59–60
previous restraint and,
50–51
previous restraint, 80
prohibition of, 70–71
printing, government control
of, 46–49
protest, right to, 18
public assembly, 71–72
public wrongs, 32–33

Rappelyea, George, 142
Raulston, John, 142, 143
R.A.V. v. St. Paul (1992), 188,
195
Reno v. American Civil Liberties
Union (1997), 18–19
revolution, right of, 91–92
rights, of individual, 29–34
Robinson, Lois, 172, 175
Robinson v. Jacksonville
Shipyards (1991), 172,
174–76
Roman Catholic Church,
11–12
Roosevelt, Franklin D., 83, 95
Roosevelt, Theodore, 77
Ross, Susan Deller, 174, 176
Roth, Samuel, 95
Roth v. United States (1957),
98–99

Sanford, Edward T., 18, 73,
147
Sanger, Margaret, 153

Saturday Press (weekly), 154
Savio, Mario, 158, 159, 161,
162–63, 166, 169
Scalapino, Robert, 166
Scalia, Antonin, 188–89, 190,
193
Schacht v. United States (1970),
111
Schenck, Charles T., 17, 77,
78, 79
Schenck v. United States
(1919), 17, 77
majority opinion in, 78–81
Schneider v. State (Town of
Irvington) (1939), 71–72
Scopes, John Thomas, 142,
144
Scopes trial, 141–44, 155
Sedition Act (1798), 16–17,
55, 62–63, 86
expiration of, 120
see also Alien and Sedition
Acts
Seebach, Linda, 194
self-government, free speech
linked with, 64–65
self-preservation,
government's right of,
84–85
sexist talk, 181–82
Sex Side of Life, The
(Dennett), 151–53
Shiell, Timothy C., 185
SLATE (Berkeley student
party), 158, 168
Smith, James Morton,
118–19
Smith Act (1940), 83, 84, 85
Socrates, 10–11
speech

is self-regulating, 23–28
public v. private forums for, 177–78
symbolic, 104–105
see also free speech; hate speech; workplace speech
Spence v. Washington (1974), 105
Stanley, Alessandra, 183
states
First Amendment applied to, 72–73
Sedition Act and control of press by, 63
Stone, Harlan, 75
Stopes, Marie, 153
Story, Joseph, 44
on liberty of press, 45–49
Street v. New York (1969), 109
Stromberg, Yetta, 153–54
Strong, Edward, 161, 168
Supplicants, The (Euripides), 10
Sutherland, George, 70–71
Sweet, Ossian, 143

Taylor, Harriet, 35
Terminiello v. Chicago (1949), 107
Texas v. Johnson (1989), 102
Thayer, James Bradley, 68
Thomas, Norman, 150
Thoreau, Henry David, 160
thought, freedom of, 39–41
Tocqueville, Alexis de, 67
Two Essays on the Liberty of the Press (Hay), 47

tyranny
liberty as protection against, 36
of the majority, 36–37
social, 37–38

Ulysses (Joyce), 153
Untermyer, Samuel, 144
UWM Post v. Board of Regents of the University of Wisconsin System (1991), 188

Vallandigham, Clement L., 17, 122–23
arrest and trial of, 126–28, 131–32
Vanderbilt, Arthur T., 145
Vinson, Frederick M., 23–24

Walker, Samuel, 140
Warren, Charles, 62, 147
Washington, George, 63
Weinberg, Jack, 160, 168
West Virginia Board of Education v. Barnette (1943), 110
Whitney, Charlotte Anita, 148
Whitney v. California (1927), 112, 179
Wilson, James, 62
Wolfson, Nicholas, 179
Woolsey, John M., 153
workplace speech, 173–74

Zenger, John Peter, 60, 117